Volume One

INTERNATIONAL LOGOTYPES

by Yasaburo Kuwayama

Rockport Publishers • Rockport, Massachusetts
Distributed by North Light Books
Cincinnati, Ohio

First published in the United
States of America by:
Rockport Publishers, Inc.
P.O. Box 396
5 Smith Street
Rockport, Massachusetts 01966
Tel: (508) 546-9590
Telex: 5106019284
Fax: (508) 546-7141

Distributed in the U.S. by:
North Light Books, an
imprint of F & W Publications
1507 Dana Avenue
Cincinnati, Ohio 45207
Tel: 1 (800) 289-0963
in Cincinnati: (513) 531-2222
Fax: (513) 531-4744

First published in Japan as
Logotypes of the World
edited by Yasaburo Kuwayama

Library of Congress cataloging
in publication data:

Kuwayama, Yasaburo
International Logotypes
Volume One

ISBN: 0-935603-41-7

Contents

Introductory Remarks

The contents of Logotypes data are as follows:

1)——Business Category
2)——Art Director
3)——Designer
4)——Client
5)——Year and Place Designed
6)——Color
→——See

All the works in this book were produced between 1970 and 1983.

Note

There are designers and copylight holders for all the marks and symbols contained in this book. Some works in this book constitute registered trademarks and are protected by law.

These works may not be reproduced without prior permission of the individual designers and copyright holders.

The Best Work From the World

This volume is a popular version of Logo Types of the World, which was originally published in A4 size as a collection of logo types produced from 1970 to 1983. Since this is a special version for the overseas market, we have selected only logo types based on roman letters. We feel that this collection, with works by 1,200 people from 34 countries, includes the best in the field from around world.

This book has been edited to contain logo types, but also includes many works with more than four characters that are more properly called trademarks. Many of these are distinctive logo-type designs, and they can be reg - istered as trademarks and protected. Many logo types in this volume were short-lived and unregistered, and this will serve as a record for those that produced them, and for others, as a useful resource for studying trends during the seventies and early eighties, sorting related works, creating new logos, and carrying out other re- search.

Though this collection may be too small a sample with which to confidently identify trends during the period, it suggests that during the period there was 1) more variety of expression, 2) use of a wider variety of script and brush styles, and 3) works that went beyond con- ventional categorization to use several or more typefaces. The first trend is evident in the logos that offered new expression by combining characters, lines, surfaces, points, and abstract or figurative objects. The second, which included a large and apparently increasing number of works, can be seen in the logos that employed calli- graphy pens, brushes, and ballpoint pens to produce attractive script. Those of the third trend often featured sans serif characters with rounded or extended and curled line ends.

Yasaburo Kuwayama

Classification and Arrangement

The special feature of this book is its grouping and categorizing of logotypes according to style. Logotypes have different styles depending on their use, content and individuality of the designer. We have tried to organize the logotypes to make them as easy to find as words in a dictionary. Because letter design is the main factor in logotypes, we used typeface style as the basis for broad categories. Roman letters were divided into (1) sans serif (2) roman, egyptian, gothic and round gothic. Following are amplifications:

Negatives & Positives: Letters are usually written in black. This is called a positive. White letters on a black background are called a negative. Examples of the two combined are 1086 and 1275.

Open & Positives: Counter line letters are called open. Examples of open combined with positives are 18, 504, 1263 and 1411.

Abbreviations: Letters in which some vertical or horizontal lines have been eliminated such as 35.

Cut-off: The whole of the letter or word is cut off by lines such as 70.

Stencil: When letters are cut out in metal plates or paper, and are used to print the letters as in 116.

Double: When part of a letter or one letter in a word is doubled as in 147.

Continuation: When letters or the word as a whole is connected as in 160.

Overlap & Contact: When letters overlap each other or touch each other as in 203.

Gradation: Regular or gradual changes. The letters in a word change from thick to thin or from dark to light or vice versa as in 251.

Strong-Weak: Words containing both strong and weak letters as in 264.

Enclosure: Those surrounded by lines such as 320 and 1292.

Tile: A combination of several surfaces with one letter on one surface as in 347.

Line: Lines added to words, parts of letters becoming lines and those with few lines such as 363 and 1301.

Inline: Letters with lines inside them such as 433.

Shadow: Letters with shadows such as 563 and 614.

Outline: Lines surrounding letters or words such as 640.

Modern: Those incorporating a new aesthetic sense such as 662.

Original: Those which have created a new style such as 743.

New: Those incorporating a new style such as 794.

Standard: Combinations of established typefaces or those close to established ones such as 879 , 1225 and 1382.

Plus α: Those incorporating simple forms, points, circles and signs, such as 897.

Plus Person: Those combined with human beings or faces such as 969 and 1323.

Plus Animal: Those combined with animals, birds, fish or insects such as 999 and 1347.

Plus Plant: Those combined with fruits, flowers, leaves and trees such as 1046 and 1349.

Plus Instrument: Those combined with tools, utensils, containers, stationery, musical instruments, cars, ships and buildings such as 1047 and 1372.

Plus Heavenly Body: Those combined with the earth, sun, and stars such as 1104 and 1113.

Sans Serif with Round Line Ends: Those equivalent to the round gothic of Japanese letters such as 1116, 1426 and 38.

Serif Gothic: Those with small serifs at line ends as in established typeface serif gothic such as 1168.

Optima: Style like established optima typeface such as 1215.

Swash: Those in which the tails or parts of letters are long or whirled such as 1448.

Ball Point Pen Script: Script with all the lines of the same thickness such as 1583.

Dot: Letters formed by dots such as 1667.

Mix: Those mixed with several typefaces as 1678.

Data: The following data were attached to each work: (1) business category: (2) art director: (3) designer: (4) year and place designed: and (5) color.

On the application forms, many people did not indicate the business category of the work. To select works according to business category, an index of these categories was established. If the art director was not specified, this space was left blank. Both names were included for joint works. The application form had a section for art director, but did not have one for director. If (2) and (3) were the same person, the name was listed twice.

The year designed was listed according to the Christian calendar. Two years were noted for cases where joint designers have submitted the work separately with two different years listed. An "R" after the year denotes that the work was redesigned in that year. An "∗" indicates the work was designed prior to 1970. These were included because they had a major influence on the works of the period, There is a year designed list for each of the classifications. Though "place designed" was not on the form, this data was included because it helps to judge where the work is being used. This was listed according the address of the person who submitted the work and to may not be accurate. To indicate the color accurately, the maker and the color number were noted in brackets after the color name.

Pantone/PMS = Pantone Co. (U.S.)
DIC = Dainippon Ink Chemical Industry (Tokyo)
TOYO CF = Toyo Ink Mfg. Co. (Tokyo)

Relationship to Trademarks

This series makes it possible to observe the different forms that trademarks and logotypes will assume. Such an advantage, however, may also present a drawback since one cannot predict in what relationship trademarks and logotypes will be employed together. Research is being conducted, particularly on their use in corporate identity.

Trademark plus logotype can express a comprehensive image. Several choices present themselves, depending upon use. To the right are single examples of many available. The combinations of trademarks and logotypes among works submitted were categorized as follows: (1) Works in which the logotype is beneath the trademark——the largest number. In many, the logotype width is the same as the trademark. Some works appear in which greater emphasis is placed on the logotype so that it is wider than the symbol, such as in T53. Others are shown in which both the logotype and trademark are given equal emphasis, such as in T60. (2) Works in which the logotype is placed above the trademark. In this pattern, the logotype is emphasized more than in (1). This pattern is used in long, horizontal spaces. There are examples of trademarks and logotypes placed on the same line to stress the horizontal, as in T91, 92, 94 and 97. (4) Works in which the logotype is to the left of the trademark. This seems to emphasize the logotype more than (3).

(5) Works in which the logotype and trademark have the same form. In these, the first letter is the trademark and the logotype is given a trademark effect simply by changing the color of the initial.

(6) Works in which the trademark and logotype are connected or similar. Examples of those with similar trademark and initial are: T109, 113, 114, and 115. Examples in which both are connected: T107 illustrates G and 4 forming a trademark. In T108, H and I combine to form a trademark. In T116 the arrow of the trademark is incorporated into the P and R of the logotype. In T117 both are formed by lines of the same thickness. In T122 the same type of spiral is used in both. There are cases such as T120 and T123 with the same curves.

1

Logotype under the trademark

T1

T2

T3

T1 1) printing
2),3) Jack Evans
4) Benetts
5) (USA)
T2 1) restaurant
2) Iwao Matsuura
3) Kenji Takumi
4) Fresh Systems
5) 1982(Japan)
6) DIC 185／DIC 156／DIC 249
T3 1) association(welfare)
2),3) Gavin Healey
4) National Foster Care
5) 1982
6) dark blue／green

7

ENPLAS

T4

Meiko

T8

SANSHIN

T12

KOVODÍLO PRAHA

T5

MODUL2

T9

seiden

T13

mamekawa

T6

NUL

T10

Shiraishi

T14

MMSD

T7

Paramount
from the heart

T11

NAPL

T15

T4 1) plastic industry
2),3) Ken´ichi Hirose
4) Daiichi Seiko
5) 1981(Japan)
6) blue
T5
2),3) Adolf Pražsky
4) Kovodilo Praha
5) 1976(Czechoslovakia)
T6 1) automobile(adjustment,
sale)
2) Osamu Ogawa
3) Hajime Fujii
4) Makekawa Jidosha
5) 1979(Japan)

T7 1) public enterprise
2),3) Kenneth Larsen
4) MMSD
5) 1977(USA)
6) blue
T8 1) trade
2),3) Ikuya Kimura
4) Meiko Shogyo
5) 1983(Japan)
T9 1) interior design
2),3) Gustavo Gomes
-Casallas／Rodorigo Fernandes
4) El Punto Del Diseño
5) 1983(Columbia)
6) red／black

T10 1) transport
2),3) Koichi Watanabe
4) NUL
5) 1977(Japan)
T11 1) stationery(greeting
card)
2) Joe Selame
3) Selame Design Group
4) Paramount Greeting Card
5) 1977(USA)
6) black or gray
T12 1) ironwork
2) Toshio Goto
3) Masahiro Hirokawa
4) Sanshin Kogyo
5) 1983(Japan)
6) black

T13 1) electric products
2) Ichro Tatsumi
3) Takeo Sugaya
4) Seiden-sha
5) 1981(Japan)
6) blue(DIC 183)
T14 1) petroleum
2),3) Ken´ichi Hirose
4) Shiraishi Shoten
5) 1981(Japan)
6) blue
T15 1) association(printing
company)
2) Joe Sonderman
3) Barry Becker／Sam Becker
4) NAPL
5) 1982(USA)
6) various color

HAKKO

T16

TRI·SEAL INTERNATIONAL INC.

T20

MANUELLA®

T24

plan west

T17

THREE QUARTERS
CREATIVE IMAGINATION

T21

U.associates

T25

RAIO

T18

INTERNATIONAL
DESIGN
FESTIVAL,
OSAKA

T22

CANCÚN

T26

TLTP

T19

PLANNING OFFICE
ADAMANT INC.
Creative Offers for Development, Management and Marketing Strategy

T23

PARMIRA CITY

T27

T16 1) construction	**T19** 1) electric parts	**T22** 1) exhibition(design)	**T25** 1) design group
2) Hajime Yoshimura	2),3) Toshiba Design Section	2),3) Takeshi Otaka	2),3) Binkou Yamauchi
3) Yoko Nonaka	4) Toshiba Kankyu Kizai	4) International Design Festival	4) U. Associates
4) Hakko	5) 1976(Japan)	5) 1982(Japan)	5) 1982(Japan)
5) 1980(Japan)	**T20** 1) printing(seal)	**T23** 1) planning office	**T26** 1) travel
T17 1) construction	2),3) Arthur Eckstein	2),3) Takahiro Shima	2),3) Joe Vera
2) Duane Wiens	4) Tri-Seal International Inc.	4) Adamant Inc.	4) Fonatur
3) Arvid Wallen	5) 1979(USA)	5) 1981(Japan)	5) 1973(Mexico)
4) Plan West	6) black	**T24** 1) clothing	6) orange/sand/pale blue
5) 1980(USA)	**T21** 1) stationery	2),3) Marlo Caroli	**T27** 1) campaign
6) rust	2) Yoichi Sugamura	4) Manuella	2),3) Takahiro Shima
T18 1) metal industry	3) Michiko Sugamura	5) 1983(Italy)	4) Parmira City
2),3) PVDI	4) Creative Imagination	6) black	5) 1979(Japan)
4) Raio	5) 1980(Japan)		
5) 1975(Brazil)	6) green/red		

American Independent Bank

T28

NCSco.,ltd.

T32

T36

TVSK

T29

LILA
yogurt bar

T33

PATRICIA
QUINTANA
Alta Cocina

T37

T30

UTÖ
VÄRDSHUS

T34

ELEKTRA

T38

GRAND DYNASTY, INC.

T31

Bahamas
Hydrofoil
Cruises

T35

arston

T39

T28 1) bank
2) Debbie McKinney
3) Mike Leidel
4) American Independent Bank
5) 1983(USA)
6) black
T29 1) publication
2),3) Milton Glaser
4) Overlook Press
5) 1983(USA)
6) black/white
T30 1) private symbol
2),3) Umberto Facchini
4) Architetti Umberto Facchini
5) 1975(Italy)
6) black

T31 1) holding company
2) Jack Evans
3) Unigraphics, Inc.
4) Grand Dynasty, Inc.
5) 1980(USA)
6) brown/blond
T32 1) interior(furniture)
2) Norihiko Watanabe
3) Mariko Ozawa
4) NCS Co.,Ltd.
5) 1982(Japan)
T33 1) restaurant
2) Iwao Matsuura
3) Takayuki Mizuno
4) Shinjuku Tokyo Kaikan
5) 1983(Japan)
6) DIC 223

T34 1) hotel(restaurant ·
recreation center)
2),3) Ove Engström
4) UTÖ Värdshus
5) 1979(Sweden)
6) dark red
T35
2),3) Silvio Gayton
4) Bahamas Hydrofoil Cruises
5) 1980(USA)
6) black/light blue/dark blue
T36 1) contest
2) Joe Vera
3) Joe Vera/Francisco Tellez
4) Turism Departamento
5) 1978(Mexico)

T37 1) school(cooking)
2) Carmen Cordera
3) Eduardo Zapata
4) Patricia Quintana Alta
Cocina
5) 1979(Mexico)
6) Pantone 209
T38 1) electrical machinery
2),3) Milton Glaser
4) Elektra
5) 1983(USA)
6) red/black/white
T39 1) record
3) Karol Sliwka
4) Foreign Polonian Enterprise
5) 1983-84(Poland)
6) black

NATIONAL CAPTIONING INSTITUTE, INC.

T40

INTERNATIONAL ORIGINAL CONCERT *in*TOKYO '81

T44

THE FOREST

T48

POL SKI TEAM

T41

avondale SWIM & TENNIS CLUB

T45

maruzen

T49

ChemJay Inc.

T42

Bank of Dallas

T46

HOTEL CHITOSEYA

T50

QuadGraphics

T43

SEADEV INC.

T47

SALON DE **SHINON**

T51

T40
2),3) Philip Gips/Diana Graham
4) National Captioning Institute, Inc.
5) 1979(USA)
6) black
T41 1) sport(team)
3) Karol Sliwka
4) Pol Ski Team
5) 1977(Poland)
6) red
T42
2) Debbie McKinney
3) Mike Leidel
4) Chemjay Inc.
5) 1982(USA)
6) blue

T43 1) printing
2) Dave Hackett
3) Ken Eichenbaum
4) Quad Graphics
5) 1974(USA)
6) black/red/yellow/blue
T44 1) festival
2) Masatoshi Shimokawa
3) Masatoshi Shimokawa/Gen Ono
4) Yamaha Music Promotion
5) 1980(Japan)
6) red/gold or black
T45 1) sport(club)
2),3) Don Connelly
4) Avondale Swim & Tennis Club
6) green

T46 1) bank
2),3) Jack Evans
4) Bank of Dallas
5) 1982(USA)
6) purple/gray
T47 1) metal industry
2) Ray Engle
3) Jerome Jensik
4) Seadev Inc.
5) 1982(USA)
6) brown/blue/black
T48
2),3) David Gibbs
4) The Forest
5) 1981(USA)
6) green

T49 1) food(manufacture)
2) Jutaro Ito
3) Koichi Kanagawa
4) Maruzen
5) 1979(Japan)
6) red
T50 1) hotel
2),3) Shin'ichi Takahara
4) Hotel Chitoseya
5) 1982(Japan)
T51 1) club
2),3) Takahiro Shima
4) Saito Shoji
5) 1983(Japan)

ROMAN

T52

BERRY BROS·PETROLEUM,INC·

T56

Courseware

T60

VENTURI

T53

ASHTON BOOKS

T57

golden pony

T61

la torre

T54

Symphony Place

T58

takeshita

T62

CALLOWHILL
Citizens Association of Reading

T55

Los Cántaros

T59

PATTERSON

T63

T52 1) shoe(sale)
2),3) Hiromi Nagano
4) Roman Juichiban-kan
5) 1981(Japan)
T53 1) jeweler
2),3) Marlo Caroli
4) Venturi
5) 1983(Italy)
6) black
T54 1) food(manufacture)
2) Carmen Cordera
3) Leticia Fierro/Fernando
Garza Galindo
4) Conservas la Torre
5) 1980(Mexico)
6) yellow(Pantone 116)/black

T55 1) association(reading)
2),3) David Bullock
4) Callowhill Citizens
Association of Reading
5) 1982(USA)
6) rust
T56 1) petroleum
2),3) Jack Evans
4) Berry Bros-Petroleum, Inc.
5) 1982(USA)
6) blue/silver
T57 1) book shop
2),3) John M. Alexander
4) Ashton Books
5) 1981(USA)
6) red

T58 1) hall
2) Tim Larsen
3) Nancy Young
4) Symphony Place
5) 1982(USA)
6) black
T59 1) restaurant
2) Juan Ignacio Gomez
3) Pedro E. Gaudiano
4) Promotora Oterera Misión
5) 1983(Mexico)
6) Pantone 484/beige
T60
2) Tom Lewis
3) Tom Lewis/Linda Roberts
4) Couresware
5) 1983(USA)

T61 1) shoe(manufacturer)
2),3) Francescco Burccini
4) Golden Pony
5) 1976(Italy)
6) blue
T62 1) food
2),3) Akira Sanada
4) Takeshita Seika
5) 1975(Japan)
T63 1) heavy industry
2),3) Jack Evans
4) Patterson
5) (USA)

GIRL SCOUTS

T64

kunimatsuya

T68

T72

FIATAGRI

T65

coni/ hairstylist

T69

Kewanee Day CAre Center

T73

T66

the piggy bank

T70

カワキン

T74

Capt'n Quick's

T67

Comanche Caves Ranches

T71

シンリョウ

T75

T64 1) organization
2) Saul Bass
3) Saul Bass／Herb Yeager
4) U. S. Girl Scouts
5) 1978(USA)
T65 1) mechanical industry
3) Carlo Malerba
4) Fiatagri
5) 1982(Italy)
6) dark red
T66 1) trading(audio)
2),3) Walter Hergenrother
4) Closina & Barpo
5) 1977(Italy)
6) red／green／black

T67 1) restaurant
2) John M. Alexander
3) Don Weller
4) Capt'n Quick's
5) 1983(USA)
6) blue
T68 1) shop
2),3) Koichi Watanabe
4) Kunimatsuya
5) 1979(Japan)
T69 1) private symbol(hair stylist)
2),3) Don Davis
4) Coni Cadi
5) 1982(USA)
6) black

T70 1) bank
2),3) Don Davis
4) Whaples Bank
5) 1977(USA)
T71
2) Jack Evans
3) Unigraphics, Inc.
4) Claud Macrahernan
5) 1980(USA)
T72 1) liquor(sale)
2),3) Ricardo Rey
4) Vinos y Quesos
5) 1980(Puerto Rico)

T73
2),3) Don Davis
4) Kewanee Day Care Center
5) 1979(USA)
6) black
T74 1) interior
2),3) Hiro Terao
4) Kawakin
5) 1983(Japan)
T75 1) rice shop
2) Jutaro Ito
3) Katsunori Hagiwara／Koichi Kanagawa
4) Shinryo Bussan
5) 1979(Japan)
6) blue

T79

2

Logotype is placed to the top of the trademark

3

Logotype is placed to the right of the trademark

T76

T80

T83

T77

T81

T84

T78

T82

T85

T76
3) Paul Ibou
4) Flag
5) 1981(Belgium)
T77 1) ironwork
3) Masahiro Shimizu
4) Seiwa Kogyo
5) 1983(Japan)
T78 1) sporting
goods(manufacturer)
2) Yoshio Nishimaki
3) Shinsuku Saito／Koji Akutsu
4) Daiichi Gosen
5) 1982(Japan)

T79 1) design studio
2) Jack Evans
3),4) Unigraphics, Inc.
5) 1972(USA)
6) black／purple
T80
2),3) Carl Nelson
4) Welsh Companies, Inc.
5) 1981(USA)
6) black／rust(PMS 159)
T81
2) Tom Lewis
3) Don Young
4) The Vault
5) 1982(USA)

T82 1) publisher
2) Concetto Pozzati
3) Maurizio Osti
4) Edizioni L'Inchiostroblu
5) 1981(Italy)
6) black／blue
T83 1) cleaner(manufacturer)
2),3) Rinaldo Cutini
4) Snia Casa
5) 1974(Italy)
6) dark blue or red or black
T84 1) excavation
2),3) Denise Spaulding
4) Robinson Excavating
5) 1980(USA)
6) green／brown

T85 1) travel
2),3) Martelossi Giovanni
4) Sharonviaggi
5) 1975(Italy)

T86

T90

4

Logotype is placed to the left of the trademark

T87

T91

T94

T88

T92

T95

T89

T93

T96

T86 1) food(frozen)
2) Rout van Den Hoed
3) Ed Sturgeon
4) Idaho Frozen Foods
5) 1977(USA)
6) blue
T87 1) sport(sale)
2) Gai Muranaka
3) Koji Takahashi
4) Sazanami
5) 1982(Japan)
T88 1) catering service
2) Alfonso Capetillo Ponce
3) Ricardo Salas
4) Grand Metropolitan
5) 1980(Mexico)
6) blue

T89 1) sporting
goods(manufacturer)
2),3) John M. Alexander
4) Alpine Products
5) 1980(USA)
6) black
T90 1) holding company
2) Joe Vera
3) Barry Cox
4) Progrupo
5) 1980(Mexico)
6) gray
T91 1) gallery
2),3) Osamu Furumura
4) Cimaise-S
5) 1974(Japan)

T92 1) theatre
2),3) Scott Engen
4) Glendale Centre Theatre
5) 1979(USA)
6) black
T93 1) hospital
2),3) Denise Spaulding
4) Bellefonte Hospital
5) 1982(USA)
6) red／black
T94
2),3) Avrum Ashery
4) Parents with Careers
5) 1981(USA)
6) black

T95
2),3) Madeleine Bujatti
4) Herbert Baginer
5) 1978(Austria)
6) blue／red
T96 1) stockbroker
2) Joe Vera
3) Joe Vera／Francisco Tellez
4) Probursa
5) 1978(Mexico)
6) brown

15

5 Logotype and trademark are the same form	 GIRO 4 T99	 The Underground Gourmet T103
 PILA T97	 HiCUT CO.,LTD. T100	G&J. GILBERT&JOHN GREENALL LTD T104
 Unicem T98	 FERRERO T101	Luoni T105
6 Logotype and trademark are connected or are similar	 Mas Cosmetics s.a T102	R ROTHSCHILD T106

T97 1) mountain association
2),3) Giovanni Burnazzi
4) Pila
5) 1979(Italy)
6) black/red
T98 1) building
material(cement industry)
2),3) Giovanni Burnazzi
4) Unicem
5) 1975(Italy)
6) gray/black
T99 1) sounding
machine(selling)
2),3) Rey R. Dacosta
4) Giro 4
5) 1978(Venezuela)
6) blue

T100 1) trading concern
2),3) Koich Watanabe
4) Hicut Co., Ltd.
T101 1) food(manufacturer)
2),3) Aldo Novarese
4) Ferrero Chocolata
5) (Italy)
6) red
T102 1) cosmetics
2),3) Tomás Vellvé
4) Mas Cosmetics s.a.
5) 1980(Spain)
6) light blue

T103 1) restaurant
2),3) Milton Glaser
4) The Underground Gourmet
5) 1966(USA)
6) black/pink/orange
T104 1) distiller and wine
merchant
2) Keith Murgatroyd
3) Keith Murgatroyd/Tony
Foster
4) Gilbert & John Greenall, Ltd.
5) 1979(England)
6) green
T105 1) manufactured goods
3) Carlo Malerba
4) Luoni
5) 1978(Italy)

T106 1) manufactured goods
2),3) Oanh Pham-Phu
4) H. Rothchild GmbH
5) 1980(West Germany)
6) gold/silver/blue

T107

T111

T115

T108

T112

T116

T109

T113

T117

T110

T114

T118

T107 1) clothing
2) Joe Vera
3) Francisco Tellez／Joe Vera
4) Emmanuelle
5) 1979(Mexico)
T108 1) air conditioning
2),3) Bror B. Zetterborg
4) Pentair
5) 1980(Finland)
6) blue
T109 1) textile
2) Alfonso Capetillo Ponce
3) Alejandro Merino
4) Texel
5) 1978(Mexico)

T110
2) Ove Engström
3) Ove Engström／Kurt
Karlsson／Ingvar Johansson
4) FFV
5) 1982(Sweden)
6) blue
T111 1) food
2) Gary Ball
3) Dave Baca
4) Bonner Packing
5) 1975(USA)
6) green／orange／black
T112 1) sports
2),3) Silvio Gayton
4) Free Port Lucaya
5) 1979(USA)
6) dark blue／light blue／yellow

T113 1) airlines
2) Jack Evans
3) Bill Oates
4) Jim Patterson Speedbird
5) 1982(USA)
T114 1) hunting and camping
supplies store
2) Jack Evans
3) Unigraphics, Inc.
4) Black Sheep
5) 1982(USA)
6) black／red
T115 1) real estate
2) Duane Wiens
3) Arvid Wallen
4) Property Investers of Colorado
5) 1983(USA)
6) gold

T116 1) real estate
2),3) G. Edwards
4) San Jemo
5) 1974(Mexico)
6) green
T117
2),3) Don L. Sterrenburg
4) Interface
5) 1974(USA)
6) brown／gray
T118 1) artists material
2),3) Binko Yamauchi
4) Ehime Gazai Co.,Ltd.
5) 1982(Japan)

T119

T122

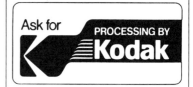

T125

T120

T123

T126

7

Designs in combinations

8

Logotype and the trademark are one and the same

T121

T124

T119 1) Japanese restaurant
2),3) Yukio Kanise
4) Masuyoshi
5) 1977(Japan)

T120 1) energy(gas)
2),3) Rodorigues Rafael
4) Comgas
5) 1971(Brazil)

T121 1) television station
2),3) Ernesto Lehfeld
4) Video 3
5) 1982(Mexico)
6) PMS 159

T122 1) automobile accessories
2) Tomoko Taketomo
3) Hisako Ogura
4) Auto Craft Anzen
5) 1982(Japan)

T123 1) restaurant
2),3) Bruce D. Zahor／Joel Mitnick
4) Pompizoo Restaurant
5) 1982(USA)
6) blue／yellow

T124
2) Shigeru Shimooka
3) Shigeru Shimooka／Toyohiko Sugimoto
4) Nichias
5) 1978(Japan)
6) dark blue／blue

T125 1) photography
2) Joe Selame
3) Selame Design Group
4) Eastman Kodak Company
5) 1983(USA)
6) black／yellow

T126 1) glass
2),3) Walter Hergenrother
4) Edilglas Production
5) 1978(Italy)
6) brown／yellow

BRÜCK
1

CONSUL
2

KEKO
7

EMERY
3

auxiliar
8

MODENA
4

COMLURB
9

OMEGA
5

ALCOR
10

1STBANK
6

FLYINGSPOT
11

12 WATTS

13 Bell

1980

15 LOBBY LOUNGE

16 JAZZ AUDIO

14 PATCHWORK & QUILTS

17 FIRE

18 BOMB

19 DISCOVERY

21 marycarter

20 NYC/AIA

22 LE PARC

23

28

24

29

25

30

26

31

27

32

21

33

34

HUEBER

35

VALESUSA

36

TRIVAS

37

FASHION

38

PRIMO FILO

39

ETOILE

40

paseo

41

LEIDEL

42

NEED

43

WEST BEND

44

U.S. TEAM

45

HARZA

46

ELAN

47

EVERY BODY

48

ZH ZÆGEL HELD

49

CASA ITALIA

50

ANGLO ENERGY

51

vétüs

52

NEWSIGN

53

TIKAL

54

KRESTMARK

55

FAKE

56

CEMA

57

RPOD

58

GIPi

59

PAINT

60

SPRINT•••

61

WERIM

62

GALERIE-in

63

CALIFORNIA

64

PROGRAPH

65

AUTO FOCUS
66

INTERMEX
68

GUERRERO CORRETORA
67

ART GRACE
69

70

amazone
71

AUSTRAL
75

COMEXPORT
72

LAZr
76

HOBBY
73

ARCARRO
77

inep
74

huerta
78

LASER TURBO SPECIAL

79

CORNELL
FORGE · COMPANY

80

81

PERMEO

82

ESPRESS

83

NEWDISC

84

anfibia

85

isolant

86

REO 2

87

DISEÑO 76

88

colorlab

89

Thunder

90

LIPCO

91

GIANT
92

OGCOATING
93

KIWI
FENCE
94

RUN
'81
The Year
Of The
Kimberly-Clark
Marathon
95

MIPOX
96

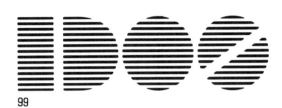
30PA
97

CANEXUS
98

IDO2
99

KEEP
100

FACSCAN
101

BARTER
UPDATE
102

PLANCAL AG
103

104

105

106

107

108

109

110

111

112

113

114

115

ELIXR

116

monica

117

A·COLLECTION

118

L·O·R·D H·O·U·S·E

119

FES''AN

120

PEGASUS

121

122

UNIVER

123

"REACT"

124

125

MEN'S-TECH

126

CAMPING BAIA DOMIZIA

127

PLA KAT

128

NITTO HOTEL
129

OASIS
130

CAMICO
131

STUDIO TECH
132

Arvan
133

New Metallic
134

Jeltek
135

OCTAV8
136

Unity
CARL PENSTAND
137

'27 HOUSE
ツー・セブンハウス
138

CATALOGUE
139

30

RAIO

140

black angel

144

GROBA

141

145

PASQUALE'S

142

REAL CAFE

143

costa

146

coffee

NOVO IMPORT

147

Carmack

148

149

156

150

157

151

152

158

EXEDRA

153

HOTEL TOHKAI

154

155

MUTUAL
AFFAIR
MUTUELLE
AMITIE

159

CALPIS

160

BIRD

161

ASWAN

162

THREE MAST

163

clamex

164

Alex Fries

165

software

166

INTERHORST

167

STAEDTLER

168

Hirex

169

FIRST

170

RSSC

REMAINS
SNOW SKI
CLUB

171

33

LIFEC
172

LIV LOVE
178

TOKO
173

TIGER
179

HGC
174

lovely
180

JAS
175

netra
181

NSP
176

arston
182

LINEA LITOS
177

BESTTIME
183

Seeker

184

Atelier Megu

185

LiLiFRiEND

186

HABA

187

SUNDEER

188

SCRF

189

PMPA

190

taktika

191

CRILAPLASTIC

192

asaf

193

HARRODS

194

PATHA'S

195

196

200

BIAOW DRUGS

197

PARK AVENUE PLAZA

198

Coopers
&Lybrand

199

THE
GLASS
OVEN

201

1400

202

203

Dialog

204

datalink

209

ZWD

205

Judgek

210

UTOPIA

206

eight CBS◉

211

NORTH AMERICAN INDIAN TRADING COMPANY

207

Light Painting

212

Disco Controller

213

TUNGSTENO HAMERA

208

Glasfast

214

DEVLIN

215

lifescape

221

SHOTGUN

216

BLACK CONE

222

TATEISHI

217

CANELA

223

GRAPHIC DESIGN

218

PowerSense

224

Aprica

219

LEYKAM

HOLZVERWERTUNGS

225

NIKLA

CELL

226

MaxField

FOR JOGGING AND RUNNING

220

MERKATOR

227

228

233

229

234

230

231

235

236

237

GRUPO

232

238

239 AMaster Athletic

246 muebles norden

240 Dairy Farm

247 BLEND

241 Soetelieve

248 Boa Boa

242 mecair

249 CALORIC MODUL

243 carshampoo

244 Plan-Do Sheet

245 BRÆGEN

250 COMBO LOOK '75

251

252

258

FONDATION NATIONALE
DE LA **PHOTO**GRAPHIE
253

259

AL**LUMIN**OX
254

CITRO**SUCO**
260

255

261

256

MINDSET
257

ORCHESTRE
DE CHAMBERY
ET DE LA **SAVOIE**
262

DANNEM**ANN**
SIE**MSEN**
BI**GLER &**
IPANE**MA MO**RE**IRA**

263

II PPRR AA

264

galerieam**züriberg**

265

JIM YARK *OLDSMOBILE /AMC*

266

Scholastic **Wizware**

267

M**EDICO** **ENGINEERING**

268

RESNAN NANZER

269

GALLERY **79**

270

SIJ B ES
& **CO** B V

271

272

273

Deutscher
Kulturrat

274

276

KLUWER
ALGEMENE
>**INFORMATIEVE**
BOEKEN BV

275

277

anil dave

278

279

280

281

282

283

284

289

285

290

286

Banco 24 Horas

291

287

PROGRAM

292

HELVEX

293

288

294

295

296

297

298

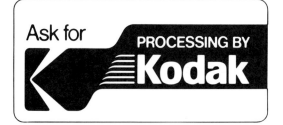

299

300

301

302

303

304

305

309

310

306

Why don't you drop by for a swim. ●Creative Pool ●03-402-3883・Jingumae, Tokyo.

311

312

307

313

308

314

315

317

319

316

318

320

321

322

Enclosure　囲み

323

324

pwn
provinciaal
waterleidingbedrijf van
noord-holland

325

326

CARL PENSTAND

327

328

329

330

331

332

333

334

339

340

335

336

341

337

342

338

343

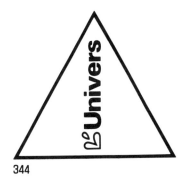

344

345

346

347

348

350

349

351

352

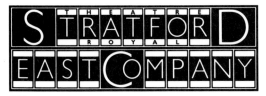
353

354

355

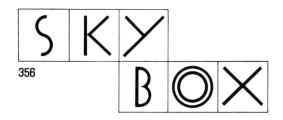
356

357

358

359

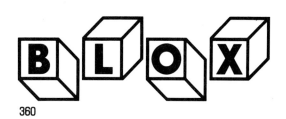
360

361

51

362

363

364

SPORTSAM

365

Bläue

367

IZUMI

366

lubric

368

SEQUENCE
369

ÖKO TEST
M A G A Z I N
375

LUNCH BOX
370

mediator
376

LANDSAT
SONY VHF/ UHF INDOOR ANTENNA
371

isomura
377

DownLights
372

JILBA RACING
378

Agropol
373

TABEC
379

APRO
374

IPANEMA
380

B&W
381

PETROBRAS
382

CORPORAÇÃO
BONFIGLIOLI
383

visual SIGN
384

NEW DANDY
385

faelba
386

CPFL
387

banespa
388

Schahin Cury
389

Morlan
390

SONNEN HERZOG
391

TOKYO SEIMITSU
392

BLEND
393

394

395

396

397

398

399

400

401

402

403

404

409

405

410

406

411

407

412

408

413

414

415

Câmara de Comércio
Líbano-Brasileira de São Paulo

416

417

418

CENTRO NACIONAL DE REFERÊNCIA CULTURAL

C | N | R | C

419

420

100 Jahre Kieler Woche

1982

19.—27.

Juni

421

422

423

429

424

430

425

426

427

428

431

Yokohama
R A G T I M E
432

433

434

438

435

436

437

439

440

441

442

calpam

448

Rhonal

443

CNC

449

bauhauS

444

metarc

445

Proa

450

446

verde

451

COLT

447

image

452

453

459

454

460

KUNZ

455

RAM

461

SKI&SKI

456

GLOBALLINK

INTERNATIONAL BUSINESS LIAISON
462

TURBO

457

SINTEMEX

458

GALA

463

TWIN21

464

469

470

BAMBOO

465

466

471

TOYOTA

467

MULTIVISION

472

468

ARONKASEI

473

Panrenty mihara

474

475

479

476

480

481

482

477

483

478

484

ROLAND
COTTON

485

КОМИТЕТ
ЗА МЛАДЕЖТА
И СПОРТА

486

APPI

487

488

489

490

491

492

493

494

495

499

500

496

501

BEAUTY BRONZE

497

mode salon

502

モード・サロン・ミュージク

498

503

504

505

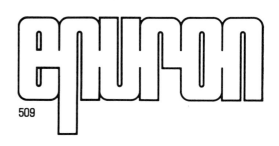

509

506

510

507

511

508

512

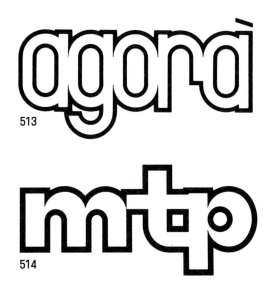

513

518

519

514

520

521

BONNE CHÈRE

515

522

·RIO·

516

EDELWEISS

517

523

524

525

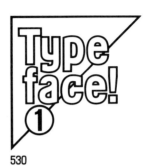

530

526

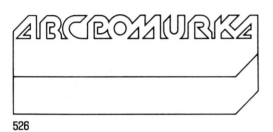

527

531

528

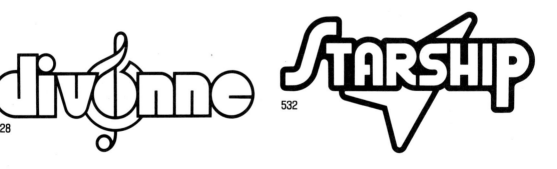

532

533

534

535

536

537

538

539

MARUWA

540

SELECTOR

541

MINICOM

542

543

544

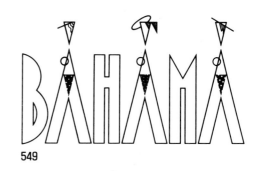

549

545

546

550

547

551 *Kizaki Design Laboratory*

548

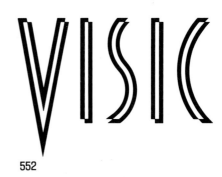

552

553

558

554

SOFTARD

559

LOFT JAZZ

555

HOT BOX

560

IMAGES

556

RESTAURANT

ROTA

561

ADAMI

557

VOICE STUDIO

562

563

564

565

566

567

568

569

СТОПАНСКИ
ХИМИЧЕСКИ
КОМБИНАТ

570

571

576

572

577

573

578

574

579

575

580

581

585

582

586

583

587

584

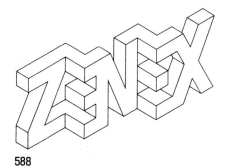

588

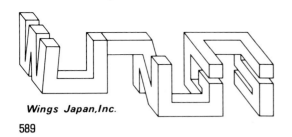

Wings Japan,Inc.

589

593

590

594

595

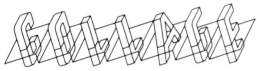

591

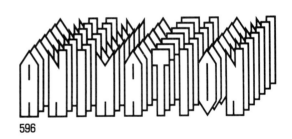

596

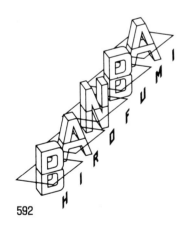

592

597

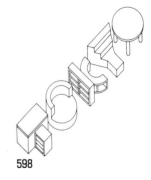

598

599

600

601

602

603

604

605

606

607

608

609

610

611

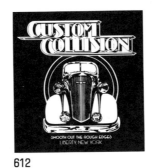

612

613

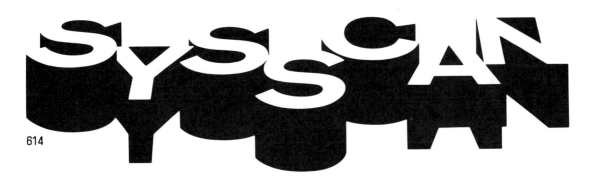

614

615

616

617

618

619

620

622

623

624

625

626

621

627

632

628

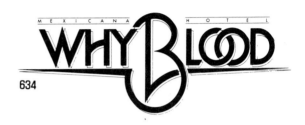

633

634

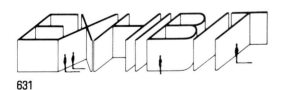

629

635

630

631

636

637

639

638

640

641

GOLDBUG

642

643

644

645

646

650

WINTER EQUIPMENTS

647

Wonderful bridge over the ocean. 19ft Cruiser by Kanematsu

651

648

652

649

653

654

658

655

659

656

660

657

661

662

663

667

664

Kobe Belle

THE
CAKE
WORLD
SINCE
1927

668

665

VisionΛge

669

666

JACQUES

670

Féege

Florin

671

THE ART &
DESIGN
HOUSE 366

366

677

marukai

672

BIWAC

678

NEWS

673

curtiss

679

TOKYO SYSTEMS CREATORS

Boxer

674

schiress

680

TURBO

675

unicef

681

FINE

MEN&WOMEN

676

adria bank ag

682

Lithium
683

Hitachi Zosen
684

Hyspan
685

CULTURE
686

SSG
687

NEWS
688

GMS·3
689

LASER
MARQUIS
TELSTAR
MUSTANG
SPECTRON
690

SORD
691

Centro
Ricerche
Fiat
692

Artifort
693

Autorama
694

JapanAsia
Airways
695

alpha
696

sansho
697

altosca
698

UNITED
699

PIAZZA
700

ENPLAS
701

Matsunaga
702

MURAYAMA
703

nimura
704

ierc
705

SKOOKUM
706

BALSECA
713

PANOLY
707

TAMSA
714

GRETAG
708

TRIP AF
709

Balloon
715

seiden
710

NiGuRa
716

Farmax
711

HOTEi
712

NAIG
717

Kakoh

718

Study House

723

LCA·J

Link Consulting Associates-Japan

719

Walserel

724

GRID

720

Banpesca

725

plantro

726

IVECO

721

Graphitec

OSAKA

727

Lipton

722

UrbanSport

FOR FASHIONABLE SPORTS LIFE

728

GAZELLE

729

CHASER

730

yamaura

731

TOTANI PRINTING

732

ACFIS
KOMPACT

733

NEMO
EUROPE

734

STUDIO ЄBIS

735

Achilles

736

WALKING·KARAOKE

737

MAGGI

738

POPULAR
science

739

ΛΛLPHΛ

740

741

742

743

MORGEN

744

747

Rabobank

745

748

=Daalderop

746

749

SYSTEMOBiL GMbH

750

JAZAUDIO
JAZADDIO

751

GANZ

752

UPh
UNZEN PARK HOTEL

753

Metal

756

GOLDEN

757

CRONVS

758

Megadex

754

yunni

759

ARBA
FILM

755

SOLTEC

760

761

765

INPUT

766

tritnrium

767

762

erekkala

768

769

t.a.p.e.s.

763

cancuncaribe

770

Dolphin

764

proposte

771

BUKOLLA

772

SCRAP

773

inatomie

774

PARCO PART3

775

PARCO+Let's

776

PAPER CLIPS

777

CHEWY

778

OIRIO

779

CRC

780

CIVIC

781

BESEDE

782

783

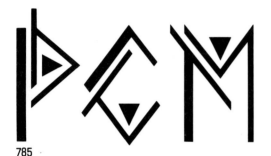

784

785

786

787

CAMARA NACIONAL DE LA INDUSTRIA CINEMATOGRAFICA

788

789

790

791

792

793

Hi·Brand
794

frosteena
795

intergrafica
796

eurografica
797

サーフライザ
surflyzer
798

ロンコム
rondrom
799

Dairy Farm
800

Parachutist
801

marco polo
802

canyon woodworks

803

French Open
ROLAND GARROS

808

yama moto

804

English today

809

MIDDLESEX COUNTY COLLEGE

805

Worker Bee ワーカービー

810

ATLANTIC

811

ТЕЛЕКОМ  **TELECOM**

806

HU)(ϾϽU

807

pochi

812

SOVPAK
ソフパック
813

SANCHEZ
819

PISCIS
820

MOSPAK
モスパック
814

HEXCEL
821

fumiya
815

DECSA
822

ZAIMA
816

GRUAS
GUANIPA CA
823

sterilite
817

Sumit's Center
824

HUBERT SAWS
818

My Thatcher's
825

CASSETTEDECK And FMAIRCHEK
826

PURE
827

ANELVA
833

ALPINE
828

NEFAX
834

DANAS
829

Wellen
835

zerocompo
836

SIGMA
830

SUNDELTA, INC.
837

SQUARE
831

DISC
838

ALPK2
832

RISING SUN
839

PAVIN
Papierveredelungsindustrie Gesellschaft m.b.H.

840

Bimbo

845

A
MILK

841

BiG STAR

846

LAURENS

847

LIVINA yamagiwa

842

Инжстрой

848

Shimaya

843

МАДАРА

849

SHIPS

1989

844

interexport

850

THE TERMINAL
851

MECANOFLEX
852

FORESIGHT-70
853

HOTELES MISION
854

LINN
855

Exciting & Elegance
856

cilsa
857

escargot
858

JASC
859

la ronde
860

BESTACK
861

DENUUA
XACKOBO
862

NOA
863

OAC
THE ORGANIZATION OF AD-CREATIVE CORPORATIONS
864

Seiwa
868

GRACE
865

produced by **Achilles**
LUX
SPORTY CASUAL
869

TOKYO BM TOPS CO.,LTD.
TOPS
866

eyes
870

VISTA
867

USHIO
871

NISSAN AIR SERVICE CO., LTD.
872

NARITA SUNNY COUNTRY CLUB
873

Japan Creative Finish Work Association
874

pik·nik foods, inc.
875

SHIKOKU TRAVEL SERVIC INC.
876

WEST RACING CARS CO.,LTD.
877

SHOWA MARUTSUTSU COMPANY, LTD.
878

BEST
879

880

881

vol.3

884

882

885

el ladril/o

883

886

Satisfied Ear Records

887

zehnder

888

Time

889

W PEACE R

890

O My Goodness! Instant Oriental Noodles

891

NATIONAL RESOURCE CENTER FOR INTERNATIONAL TRADE EDUCATION

894

THE SUMMIT

892

NATIONAL INTERPRETER CONSORTIUM TRAINING

895

cuadrifolio cuadrifolio cuadrifolio cuadrifolio

893

libreria a·zeta

896

BOSTONIAN

897

898

B®ANDS

899

cyclotronic

900

O kray's

901

902

HBO
Premiere Films

903

AUDIO FAIR '82

904

optical company

905

**Baumann,
Koelliker AG**
906

912

Polfin
907

Shibuya
913

ERTOIL
Lubricantes
908

sandpebbles
914

PrairieOil
909

915

E-Z-SCAPE
910

DIXIE
916

PARISIAN
911

K I N D W E A R
917

918 NATURAL HEALTH FOODS

923

919

924

920

925

921

926

922

927

928

929

934

930

935

931

936

932

937

933

938

939

940

941

942

943

COMPUTER
SEARCH

944

プラスα　Plusα

946

Communications

947

Medicina

948

949

RIPOSATE

950

951

945

952

957

953

958

959

954

Rendez-vous avec la France !

960

955

961

2000 JAHRE AUGSBURG

962

Strømme

956

963

964

965

966

967

968

969

970

971

Person 人

972

977

studio
ワン・ルームスタジオ

973

Teatro Estable Castellano

978

974

979

975

976

980

981

982

983

984

985

986

987

CASA OLIMPICA

988

989

990

991

995

992

996

993

997

994

998

999

114

1000

1004

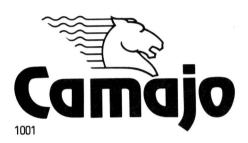

1001

1005

1002

1006

1003

1007

1008

こびこばこち

1009

1010

Planatec

1011

1015

PR**O**JECT
PRIDE

1012

Dolphin

1016

K**O**NG

1013

Voyager

1017

SAFETY
and FAST

1014

FORMFIT

1018

1019

Mary
Jane

tangerine
1020

STYLISTOREP.
1021

NEWHERD iN NEWYORK
1022

OSAWA
1023

MARPHA
APPLES
1024

ALMOND PLAZA
1025

THE
FOOD
BANK
1026

FRUIT PARLOUR
mine
1027

KOSHIji
1028

Spring Special
1029

1030

1036

1031

1037

1032

1033

1038

1034

1039

1035

1040

1042

1041

1044

1043

1046

1045

1047

1048

1049

1050

1054

1051

1052

1055

1056

1053

le vie sung
cucina asiatica a casa vostra
1057

1062

1058

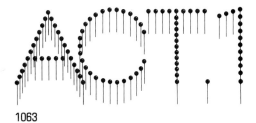

1063

1059

1064

1060

1065

1061

Plus Instrument　道具

1066

1067

1068

1069

1070

1071

1072

1073

1074

1075

1076

1077

1078

1081

OOL SAN ANGEL

1082

Fix'm!

1083

ad.angle

1084

1079

SKI TRAIN

1080

1085

1086

SHIRTIQUE

1087

1088

123

Plus Instrument　道具

1089

1094

1090

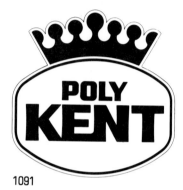

1091

1095

POLY
KENT

MISSION BIOFORCE DEVELOPPEMENT

1096

1092

1093

GRAND
CENTRAL
RACQUETBALL
CLUB

1097

道具/天体　Plus Instrument/Plus Heavenly Body

1098

1101

1099

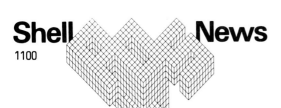

1102

Shell
1100

1103

SOCINTER

1104

1105

1106

1107

1108

1112

1113

1109

1114

1110

1111

1115

1116

1117

GALANT

1118

Marielou

1119

Witty

1120

Penny

1121

1122

STUDIO LAMBERT

1123

1124

APPLY3

1125

NEO CONCEPTUAL SPACE
METAFA
1126

BROT HAUS
1127

Mas Cosmetics s.a
1128

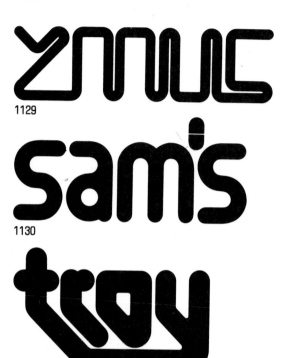
1129

imai
1134

sam's
1130

ZIGZAG
1135

troy
1131

RIVERO
1136

EXICOM
1137

1132

MON PAIN
1133

helio
1138

128

GOLLER G

1139

PICNÍQUE

1140

HARIO

1141

OFFSHOOT

1142

AEROTOPO

1143

Hello City

1144

Lukubu

1145

Happy tree

1146

THEROS

1147

ORIVEO

1148

Copi Copi

1149

Whip&Whip

1150

mojuran

1151

popstitch

1152

1153

1154

1155

1156

1157

1158

1160

1161

1159

1162

1163

Smile to smile

1164

1166

CHICO'S
MEXICATESSEN

1165

NUOTO IMPERI

1167

dyslexia

BOLTON & DISTRICT DYSLEXIA ASSOCIATION

1168

Check&Save

1169

CRISTO
EN
1970

1171

St.STEPHEN'S

1170

EUROPEAN

1172

131

OKAHASHI

1173

TOKAI TV PROMOTIONAL
LITHO SERIES

1174

SUPER NIKKA

1175

LIVING FASHION
YELLOW HOUSE

1176

R·nubo

Remote control New Unique Body Object
1177

ULTRA
Bauzentrum

1178

come for a chat
ALBION
SANDWICH and TEA GARDEN

1179

BACKDOOR

ART GALLERY/21 SOUTH MOGER AVE /MT KISCO NY (914) 666-6064

1180

Snack & Café Lounge
HERMES
24
TJLXZ

1181

Baglow
Harris West &
partners

1182

KISKADEE
FABRICS Ltd.

1183

1184

1188

1189

1185

1190

1186

1191

1187

1192

1193

1194

91.5fm

1195

SLICK

1196

J·PRICE

1197

1198

1199

TEQUILA.

1200

GIN.

1201

1202

ICHIRINO
KOGEN HOTEL

1203

1204

1209

I.M.T. CORP.

1205

1210

W🞔RLD PLAN

1206

1207

1211

1212

1208

1213

1214

SCORE
1215

ALOS
1216

Doji House
1217

GUTHMANN
1218

BRÆGEN
1219

CREDICARD
1220

1221

1222

1223

PHAROS
1224

1225

DEMI SAISON
1226

edilipa edilipa
1227

SAISON
1228

HANAE MORI
INTERIOR FABRICS
1229

...ing.
1230

Juel Vérité Ohkubo
1231

LucioViezzoli&C
1232

Ward Howell
1233

Galaxis
1234

ART as applied to medicine
1235

Salle Pleyel
1236

30 posters
1237

137

GALLERY

1238

RHINE CELLAR

1245

CAFÉ-TERRASSE
LUMIÈRE
1239

CANARDEAUX
1246

Rose moon
1240

COLLECTION
SOFIERE
1247

Importer
1241

Danaè
1248

SZEANSZ
1242

Again
1249

SnoWest
1243

BERNARD'S
1250

ROYAL COURSE
1244

138

mc Sister
1251

TOPOS
1257

RECORD SHOP
ARS
1252

The
Tournament
1258

Vert
Ohsho Chlorella
1253

STRASSEL'S
1259

Salita
1254

Mursika
1260

Knit
1255

Family
gift
1261

JOMON
1256

ARCHIA
1262

Alitalia

1263

MASAKAZU TANABE

1264

HAUS DIETLER

1265

Instituto de Análise
de Comportamento

1266

MAISON
de
FRANCE

1267

CUP NOODLE
CHICKEN
NOODLE
チキンヌードル

1269

HOBBIES&
MODELS

1268

Guiso

1270

THE CLUB
AT THE WORLD
TRADE CENTER

1271

1272

1273

Greengrass Gallery

1274

1275

1276

1277

1278

1279

1284

1280

1285

1281

1286

1287

1282

1283

1288

1289

1290

1297

1291

1294

1298

1292

1295

1299

1293

1296

1300

R·U·G·G·E·R·O
R·A·I·M·O·N·D·I

1301

NEVILLE-
SARGENT
GALLERY

1302

The D*esign* Index

1303

BOLLA
Brut

1304

HAUTE·AYER
ADVERTISING · PUBLIC RELATIONS

1305

EARLY ON

1306

Swing
music•pub

1307

infomar

1308

The
Heat
Machine

1309

SATURNIA

1310

BECHET'S

1311

ATALLA

1312

D'Velvet

1313

eye's eye

1314

HOTEL

EDEN ROC

MIAMI BEACH

1316

ZOETROPE STUDIOS

1315

METAL

RESTAURANT & BAR

1317

DOLLAR STOCK JOURNAL

1318

PAPER FOR PENS

1320

JAZZ!

LIVE • FROM • TROLLEY • SQUARE

1319

Preview

An Educational Publication from Instructional Media Services

1321

MY CITY

1322

1328

1323

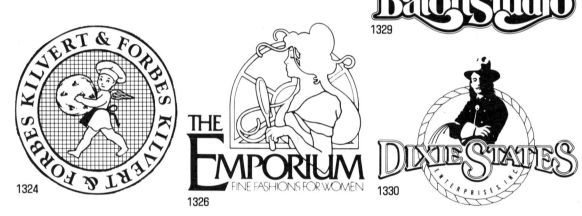

1329

1324

1326

1330

1325

1327

1331

GRITOS & SUSURROS

Todo en Sonido S.A.

1332

Primavera'80

SHIGEO
KATSUOKA

1337

CAFE DEL

MINOTAURO

1338

VERA KOPP

1333

STEEPLE CHASE

1339

HEARTLAND
MARKET

1334

LA LLUNA
I LA PRUNA

1340

ROBBA

1335

MILLER & SCHWEIZER
1336

la Cachette

1341 RESTAURANT & PUB

147

1342

1343

1344

1345

1346

1347

cerise

1348

1349

PERSIMMON PRODUCTIONS

1350

1351

1352

RESTAURANT　MACROBIOTIC

1357

1358

1353

THE
IN THE SKY

1354

1355

WINDOWS ON THE WORLD

1356

1359

《フローレット》パート2

1360

1361

1362

149

1363

1367

1368

1364

HIROSHIMA BATON

1369

Royal ♛ Care

1365

1370

corɜnas

1366

1371

1372

1374

1376

1373

1375

1377

1378

1379

1380

1381

Pit-in

1382

dialog

1383

from Cluett

1384

Industrial Structures

1385

Voice

1386

SX-100

1388

Intradal

1389

1390

ADAPTIVE TEST

1387

1391

TOWA

1392

BAJA INN

1393

Quicky

1394

JMPS

1395

Cobbler's Bench

1396

SIGNUM

1397

BANDASHA

1398

MAGIC CIRCUS

1399

ABCDEFGRA
PHIX HOUSE,
INC.DEFGHIJ
KLMNOPQRS
TUVWXY&Z

1400

Wissenschaftsladen
Ein Bürgerservice
an der Universität Bielefeld
Tel. 106-4914   Mo-Fr 16-19 Uhr

1401

EMHART
REPORT

1402

БЪЛГАРСКИ ДЪРЖАВНИ ЖЕЛЕЗНИЦИ

1403

INKPOT

1406

DIESEL *Multi*

1404

Parlour MAUPITI

1407

NORTH AMERICAN NEWSTIME

1405

MITSUBA

1408

CANADA

1409

Petits Champs-Élysées

1410

HARLAND'S FIRST TEAM

1411

BRUGE

1412

OH-HO

1413

EXPLAN

1414

1415

1420

1421

1416

1422

ASPEMAR

1417

The first choice

1423

TFC Foods Ltd

MEPHISTO

1418

BRINGING UP

1424

1419

1425

CrunchPads

1426

M miracle MENU

1427

BiEL:

1433

"Oh! My Dining"
〈オー・マイ・ダイニング〉

1428

nuclear off.

1434

Fashion Current

1429

momente

1435

● Matsuzakaya
ginza5

1430

(.,:;'?"The)
LEMONT
GARAGE
GASOLINE
KEROSENE
AND SEC-
RETARIAL
SERVICES
(.,:;'"!*?-)

1436

M I C H E L

1431

F O L L I E T

KALBRO

1432

BetterHalf

1437

1438

1439

1440

1441

1443

1444

1445

1442

1446

1447

1448

Delikate

1452

COFFEE HOUSE TOLEDO

1449

Kari Kari Hakase

1453

Mycana

1450

A merry Christmas to you

1454

Ven·dall

1451

Canon Annual 1981

1455

A.J. Wright AND SONS LTD.

1456

ROPPONGI'S DISCO WITH A DIFFERENCE

XANADU

1457

montparno

1458

1459

1460

1461

1462

1463

1464

1465

1466

1467

1468

1469

1470

1475

1471

1476

1472

1477

1473

1478

1474

1479

1480

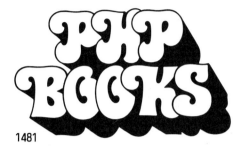

1481

1482

1483

1484

1485

1486

1487

1488

1489

Lui Chantant
PRODUCED BY WORLD CO.,LTD.

1490

Mercurey

1491

Royal Northern College of Music

1492

Domäne Geisenheim am Rhein

1493

Federico Benegas

1494

La Taste

1495

Jack and Betty PACKAGE BOUTIQUE

1496

Hotel New Yunohama Resort

1497

KONDITOREI CAFÉ
Mozart

1498

Museum

1499

Fujimido

1500

Imprimerie Papeterie de la Jumène

1501

1502

1507

1503

1508

1504

1509

1510

1505

1511

1506

1512

1513

1514　FASHIONABLE BEST QUALITY BOOTS **COSSACKY** BY **Achilles**

1518

1515

1519

1522

1523

1516

1520

1524

1517

1521

1525

Alpen Zauber

1526

Calligraphie

1531

CASAVANT

1527

Cafeteria

1532

Pancho Fierro

1528

מיפועײן

1533

Soleil des Nations

1529

la Crêperie

1534

Beauté Éterna

1530

Griffin's
RESTAURANT

1535

1536

1543

1537

1538

1539

1540

1541

1542

1549

1550

1551

1552

1553

Harris'

1554

Sonogi

1556

Beck

1555

Bonforét

HIGH QUALITY CAKES

1557

Sunshine Scandal

1558

167

1559

1560

1561 MISS Takao

1562

1563

1564

1565

1566

1567

1568

1569

1570

1571

1572

1573

1574

1575

1576

1577

1578

1579

1580

1581

1582

Fine food, spirits and all that jazz

Primo
BOTTEGA DEL VINO
1583

The Brooklyn Hospital
1584

jazz
1585

Sweet Sugar
1586

movie
1587

We ♥ caty
1588

Ponte
SEIKO
1589

Acatex
1590

newwork
1591

Lutece
1592

1593

Cactus

1594

Italiano

Musique

1595

Poésie

C. Baudelaire 1821 - 1867
Il faut être toujours ivre. Tout est la.

1596

GREEN CAMEL

1597

Sky Bird

1598

Fiorucci

1599

Zun

1600

Texas Bar

1601

TOMATO & LEMON

Love Doubles

1602

Soft & Mellow

1603

●FINE FOODS

Hisacy

MATOBA HIROSHIMA 082-263-0093

1604

Gestetner

1605

171

RED HOT EXPRESS

1606

Cheek to Cheek

1612

Blend

1607

The Parlance

1608

new yamaha audio

1613

JAZZ CALENDAR 98

1609

THE Subway

1614

Shear Sensations

1615

Gallery

1616

Wonderful Robe

1610

Rock'n House

1611

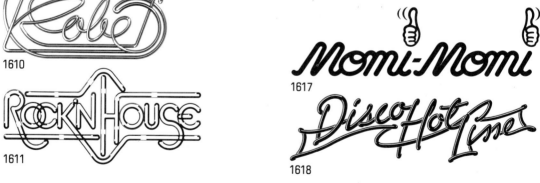

Momi-Momi

1617

Disco Hot Line

1618

1619

1624

The Evening Post

1625

homo

1620

Imprimerie Pantinoise

Bureaux / 6, Cité du Labyrinthe
75020 / PARIS / Tél. 797.29.19 +
(Entrée) / 24 rue de Ménilmontant)

1626

BAR

1621

Dichter

1627

Revolution

CASUAL WEAR
PRODUCED BY KOLBO CO., LTD.

1622

FIRINO-MARTELL

1628

Hotell Selma Lagerlöf

1623

EROS

1629

1630

1634

1631 Rodopa

1635

1632 JoliChapeau

1636 MAGALI

1633 bebesit

1637 AGTUM

1638 J

W

▲

I

1639

1642 RESOURCE1

1640

1643 GONTRAN

1641 PerkyJean

1644 BOSCA

BAR
BUDUR

1645

Le JOUR

où nous serons maîtres chez nous

1651

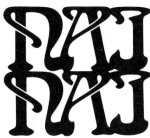

1646

ÉXPO MÚSICA

1652

STAGE

1653

CAIRN

1647

PORTABLE
KEYBOARD

1654

NOANOA

ナイトクラブ・ノアノア

1648

CHOCARD

1649

CORRIDOR

1655

mrs birds

1650

elton

1656

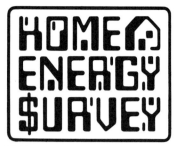

1657

1663

CHEF MATE

1658

CHARDON

1664

ROUX BOUILLON

1659

ECLAT

1660

s námi každý den plný pohody

1665

Yum Yum!

1661

1662

1666

1667

1668

Bockman

1669

TheSquare

1670

UNICK

1671

IMPACTO

1672

1673

FLASH
POINT

1674

1675

1676

ANDREA JAKIL
1677

1678

P'Beatcehr
1679

SAX FANTASY
1680

MUSIC POWER NOW!
1681

1682

1683

1684

1685

1686

Logotype Variations

Logotypes vary, of course, depending upon need. Viewing distance will determine size——large from far away and growing smaller as proximity and paper size decrease. In the larger logotype, the lines appear thin and weak. In smaller sizes, the details will disappear. Consequently, those with thick lines are used when placing logotypes on buildings or neon signs. Thinner lines will be used on business cards, stationery, etc. Logotypes with lines of two or three different thicknesses become necessary to present a constant image.

Often—seen logotypes are used also as decorations. At company reception desks, logotype variations express the individuality of the company or the atmosphere of the reception area. Choices may be made by selecting among open types, types cut with a line, three dimensional and moving types. Some incorporate light and shadow into the design. Naturally, the designer will create specific effects for his client.

Shown here are variations of one logotype. No details are available of how they are being used.

T127 1) publication
3) Miloš Ćirić
4) Danas
5) 1983(Yugoslavia)

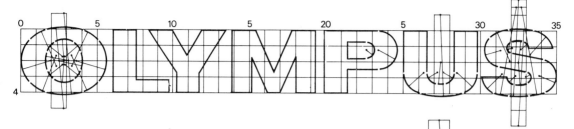

Indexing Diagram for Logotype

When writing a logotype on a big wall surface, a diagram to show how to index the letters becomes necessary.

The indexing diagram shows the proportion between right and left, and top and bottom of the logotype. It also indicates the size of letters, space between letters, thickness of lines, and the positions and centers of circular arcs.

T128 1) camera manufacturer
2) AD-Olympus Optical
3) D-Yasaburo Kuwayama
4) Olympus Optical Industry
Co.,Ltd.
5) 1979(Japan)

Artists and their Works

Artists and their Works

Artists and their Works

Index

2),3) Gerd Leufert
4) Sesus Soto
5) 1981(Venezuela)
6) black
111
2),3) Silvio Coppola
4) Transair
5) 1969(Italy)
112 1) railway jubilee
2),3) Georg Staehelin
4) Organizationskomitee '100 Jahre Eisenbahn im Glarnerland'
5) 1979(Switzerland)
6) black
113 1) walking shoes
3) Helmut Schmid
4) ASICS
5) 1983(Japan)
114 1) beauty salon
2) Yoichi Sugamura
3) Michiko Sugamura
4) Five-Avenue
5) 1983(Japan)
115
2),3) Hans Weber
4) Sobo Ernstbollag AG
5) 1977(Switzerland)
6) gray →M3
116 1) cosmetics
2) Shunsaku Sugiura
3) Helmut Schmidt
4) Shiseido
5) 1983(Japan)
117 1) private symbol(designer)
2) Félix Beltrán
3) Mónica Reyes
4) Mónica Reyes
5) 1983(Mexico)
6) deep orange
118 1) art gallery
2),3) Takenobu Igarashi
4) A-Collection
5) 1982(Japan)
119 1) men's suit(brand)
2) Hideki Kihara
3) Akisato Ueda
4) 3M
5) 1983(Japan)
120 1) shop in a station building
2) Kyodo Yamaguchi
3) Katsuaki Inagaki／Kazunari Nishida
4) Fesan in Morioka Terminal Building
5) 1980(Japan)
121 1) international seminar
2),3) Harumasa Misaki
4) International House of Japan
5) 1983(Japan)
122 1) restaurant
2),3) Tadasu Fukano
4) Karuizawa Prince Hotel
5) 1974(Japan)
123 1) sporting goods(manufacturer)
2),3) Yoshimitsu Kato
4) Univer
5) 1983(Japan)
6) green(DIC 388)／light green(DIC 211)
124 1) fiberglass(manufacturer)
2),3) Terry Lesniewicz／Al Navarre
4) Owens-Corning Fiberglas

5) 1981(USA)
125 1) electrical appliances
2),3) Allan W. Miller
4) ALTA TENSION
5) 1980(USA)
6) red
126 1) department store(boy's wear shop)
3) Yutaka Mitani
4) Seibu Dept. Stores
5) 1980(Japan)
127 1) campground
2),3) Alfredo de Santis
4) Baia Domizia
5) 1978(Italy)
128 1) entertainment (exhibition)
2),3) Gert Wunderlich
4) Gert Wunderlich's Private Exhibition
5) 1976(West Germany)
6) black
129 1) resort hotel
2),3) Ken'ichi Kaneko
4) Nitto Kogyo
5) 1977(Japan)
130 1) record
2),3) Oanh Pham-Phu
4) Giorgio Moroder
5) 1974-75(West Germany)
6) green／ochre
131
2),3) David Gibbs
4) Camco
5) 1979(USA)
6) blue
132 1) department store(the personal computer department)
2),3) Yoriya Ueda
4) Seibu Dept. Stores
5) 1980(Japan)
133 1) health food
2),3) Yoshihiro Kishimoto
4) Arvan
5) 1982(Japan)
134 1) car wax
2),3) Yoshihiro Kishimoto
4) Wilson
5) 1982(Japan)→C31
135 1) construction
2),3) Gavin Healey
4) Jeltek Limited
5) 1970(England)
6) red→M1
136 1) entertainment (exhibition)
2),3) Gavin Healey
4) Octavo
5) 1972(England)
6) purple／red→C28
137 1) office supplies
2),3) Yoshihiro Kishimoto
4) Carl Office Equipment
5) 1977(Japan)
138 1) department store (casual interior department)
2) Yoriya Ueda
3) Hidekazu Honda
4) Seibu Dept. Stores
5) 1980(Japan)
139 1) catalogue of steel tools
3) Yutaka Sato
4) Miyagi Steel Tools
5) 1980(Japan)
140 1) metalworking industry

2),3) PVDI
4) Mattheis Indústrias Metalúgicas Produtos Raio
5) 1975(Brazil)
141 1) bread(making)
3) Rosmarie Tissi
4) Groba
5) 1971(Switzerland)
6) ochre
142 1) restaurant(pizza)
2),3) Harry Murphy
4) Pasquales
5) 1975(USA)
6) brown／reddish brown
143 1) coffee manufacturer
2),3) PVDI
4) Realcafé
5) 1971(Brazil)
144 1) theater
2) John Follis
3) Jean-Claude Muller
4) Marc Taper Forum
5) 1978(USA)
6) black
145
2),3) K. C. Jones
4) Carbon Copy
6) violet
146 1) coffee
2) Fernando Rión／Jorge Carral
3) Fernando Rión
4) Costa Coffee
5) 1977(Mexico)
6) white／warm red
147 1) trade
2),3) Claude Dietrich
4) Novo Import
5) 1980(Peru)
6) black／red
148
2),3) Don Davis
4) Carmack／Wyoming
5) 1975(USA)
6) black
149 1) magazine
2),3) James Lienhart
4) Share
5) (USA)
150 1) construction
2),3) Ernesto Lehfeld
4) Techint
5) 1974(Mexico)
6) PMS 548
151 1) computer network
2) Yoshio Tsuda
3) Takaaki Yoshinobu
4) NEC Corporation
5) 1983(Japan)
152
2),3) Toru Sakuma
4) Kuraflex
5) 1983(Japan)
6) yellow green(Pantone 376C)／dark green(Pantone 378)
153 1) telephone
3) Toru Sakuma
4) NEC Corporation
5) 1982(Japan)
154 1) hotel
2) Adomondo
3) Naoto Ishikawa
4) Hotel Tohkai
5) 1983(Japan)
6) black／green
155 1) commercial company

3) Tsuyokatsu Kudo
4) Wonderful World Co.,Ltd.
5) 1977(Japan)
6) golden red
156 1) men's wear
2) Osamu Furumura
3) Yasuhiro Nakamura
4) Gunze
5) 1983(Japan)
157 1) printing
2),3) Yoshihiro Yoshida
4) Soin
5) 1981(Japan)
158 1) sporting goods
2),3) Yasuko Takeda
5) 1976(Japan)
159
2),3) John S. Brown
4) Mutual Life of Canada
5) 1972(Canada)
6) blue／green
160 1) food
2) Takenobu Igarashi
3) Takenobu Igarashi／Hiroshi Asami
4) The Calpis Food Industry Co.,Ltd.
5) 1982(Japan)
161 1) design office
3) Kazuharu Fujii
4) Bird Design
5) 1977(Japan)
162 1) upholstery
2),3) Akira Hirata
4) Daiso
5) 1973(Japan)
163 1) television program production
2),3) Eita Shinohara
4) Three Mast
5) 1981(Japan)
164 1) food(canned provisions)
2),3) Allan W. Miller
4) CLAMEX
5) 1979(USA)
6) magenta
165
2),3) Stan Brod
4) Alex Fries Company
5) 1979(USA)
6) dark green
166 1) computer package
2) Shun'ichi Horiuchi
3) Masahiro Toki
4) NEC Corporation
5) 1983(Japan)
167
2),3) Ettore Vitale
4) Interhorst
5) 1979(Italy)
168 1) stationery(materials)
2),3) Manfred Wutke
4) Staedtler-Mars
5) 1973(West Germany)
6) blue
169 1) portable exhibition for hire
2),3) Tony Forster
4) Hirex
5) 1970(England)
6) red／brown
170 1) sculpture group
2),3) Yukihisa Takakita
4) Group First
5) 1978(Japan)
171 1) ski club

5) 1981(Japan)
6) red
230 1) city
3) Eduard Prüssen
4) City of Bergisch Gladbach
5) 1975(West Germany)
6) black
231 1) cleaning supplies
2),3) Jorge Sposari
4) Limpex
5) 1977(Argentina)
232 1) construction
2),3) Fernando Rión
4) Grupo Corf, S.A.
5) 1981(Mexico)
6) red(Pantone 485C)
233 1) hair products
2),3) Fernando Rión
4) Clairol de México
5) 1978(Mexico)
6) gold/orange(Pantone 513C)
234 1) small articles(retail trade)
2),3) Mick Brain Center
4) Cosmic
5) 1983(Japan)
235 1) fashion
2),3) Alfonso Capetillo Ponce
4) Hazzard, S.A.
5) 1978(Mexico)
6) green
236 1) electronics
2) João Carlos Cauduro/
Ludovico Antonio Martino
4) Digirede(Sistemas de
Informacção)
5) 1980(Brazil)
237
2),3) Gil. L. Strunck
4) Barrage
5) 1979(Brazil)
6) blue/green
238 1) electronic industry
2),3) Christof Gassner
4) Schaar Electronic Co.,Ltd.
5) 1983(West Germany)
6) black
239 1) shoes(making, selling)
2) Nobuyoshi Nakanishi
3) Yoshio Hirano
4) Achilles
5) 1982(Japan)
6) blue/red
240
2),3) Henry Steiner
4) Dairy Farm Co.,Ltd.
5) 1982(Hong Kong)
6) red/blue
241
3) Daphne Duijvelshoff
4) Soetelieve
5) 1979(Netherland)
6) blue→C30
242 1) air compressing
business
2) Massimo Dradi
3) Aldo Travagliati
4) Mecair
5) 1976(Italy)
6) black
243 1) chemical products
2),3) Tetsuo Noda
4) Dia Chemical
5) 1975(Japan)
244 1) business diary
2),3) Hiroshi Toida

4) Japan Efficiency Association
5) 1979(Japan)
245 1) computer(hardware)
2) Marty Neumeier
3) Sandra Higashi
4) The Braegen Corporation
5) 1983(USA)
6) gray
246 1) interior(furniture
manufacturer)
3) G. Edwards
4) Muebles Norden
5) 1978(Mexico)
6) brown
247 1) artist
2),3) Masayuki Yano
4) Polystar record
5) 1982(Japan)
248 1) accessory shop
2),3) Shuji Torigoe
4) Toko Business Concern
5) 1982(Japan)
249 1) trade(fireplace export)
3) István Szekeres
4) Ferunion
5) 1981(Hungary)
6) white/black
250 1) title of a magazine
article
2),3) Shigo Yamaguchi
4) Swing Journal Co.,Ltd.
5) 1975(Japan)
251
2),3) Armin Vogt
4) Cilag Co., Ltd.
5) 1982(Switzerland)
6) black
252. 1) broadcasting
2),3) Giovanni Brunazzi
4) Itedi
5) 1981(Italy)
253 1) photography
2),3) R & S Baur
4) Fondation de la
Photographie
5) 1982(Switzerland)
6) black→M20
254 1) aluminium
2),3) Giovanni Brunazzi
4) Gruppo Bodino
5) 1979(Italy)
255 1) security trust
2) Gottschalk & Ash
International
3) Peter Adam/Stuart Ash
4) Security Trust Company
5) 1977(Canada)
256 1) food
2),3) Stephan Kantscheff
4) Bulgarkonserv
5) 1977(Bulgaria)
257
2),3) Michael Vanderbyl
4) Mindset Corporation
5) 1983(USA)
6) black/white
258 1) data processing
2) Keith Murgatroyd
3) Tony Forster
4) Modac Data Systems Ltd.
5) 1982(England)
6) gray
259 1) loudspeaker
(manufacturer)
2),3) Christof Gassner

4) Canton
5) 1974(West Germany)
6) black
260 1) juice(manufacturer)
3) Rodrigues Rafael/Beatriz
Araújo/Nair Iannibelli
4) Citrosuco S.A.
5) 1981(Brazil)
6) yellowish red/green
261 1) title of a magazine
article
2) Kuniharu Masubuchi
3) Hiroshi Iseya
4) Mikimoto
5) 1981(Japan)
262 1) orchestra
2),3) R & S Baur
4) Orchestre de Chambéry
5) 1981(Switzerland)
6) black
263
2),3) PVDI
4) Dannemann/Siemsen/
Bigler/Ipanema Moreira
5) 1972(Brazil)
264
2),3) Michael Baviera
4) IPRA
5) 1974(Switzerland)
6) black
265
2),3) R & S Baur
4) Gallery at Züriberg
5) 1981(Switzerland)
6) Ultramarine Blue
266
2),3) Terry Lesniewicz/Al
Navarre
4) Jim Yark Oldsmobile
5) 1983(USA)
267 1) children's
computer(software)
2) Robert P. Gersin
3) Johann Schmacher/Scott
Bolestridge
4) Scholastic
5) 1983(USA)
6) black or white→C142
268 1) engineering
3) Peter Skalar
4) Medicoengineering
5) 1975(Yugoslavia)
6) black
269
2),3) R & S Baur
4) Stempel and Gravurgeschäft
5) 1981
6) gray/red
270 1) art gallery
2),3) Yukihisa Takakita
4) Gallery 79
5) 1979(Japan)
271 1) accountant
2),3) H. W. Lohman
4) Sijbes & Co.
5) 1981(Netherlands)
6) black
272
2) Stankowski & Duschek
3) Anton Stankowski
4) Bayern Versincherung
5) 1977(West Germany)
273 1) education
2) Keith Murgatroyd
3) Tony Forster

4) University of Salford
5) 1982(England)
6) black/red
274
2) Helmut M. Schmidt-Siegel
3) Helmut M. Schmidt-Siegel/
Klingen
4) Deutscher Kulturrat
5) 1983(West Germany)
6) black/dark red
275 1) publishing
2),3) Donald Patiwael
4) Kluwer Publishers
5) 1982(Netherlands)
6) blue/black
276
2) Gottschalk & Ash
International
3) Stuart Ash
4) Kates, Peat Marwick & Co.
5) 1971(Toronto)
277 1) title of a photograph
collection
2) Masataku Ara
3) Taijiro Nakayama
4) Masataku Ara's Photograph
Office
5) 1979(Japan)
278 1) private symbol
(photographer)
2),3) Sudarshan Dheer
4) Anil Dave
5) 1980(India)
6) black
279 1) public agency
2),3) Dicken Castro
4) Ministry of Public Works
and Transportation
5) 1980(Colombia)
6) black
280 1) Industry
2) Joe Selame
3) Selame Design Group
4) Ludlow Corporation
5) 1972(USA)
6) blue(PMS 300)
281 1) wood-fiber boards
2),3) Elsa Pfister
4) Pavatex Co.,Ltd.
5) 1968(Switzerland)
6) green
282 1) service station
2) Joe Selame
3) Selame Design Group
4) Amoco(Standard Oil of
Indiana)
5) 1981(USA)
6) red/white/blue/black
283
2),3) PVDI
4) Zillo Lorenzetti
5) 1969(Brazil)
284 1) confection
2),3) Gustavo Gomez
-Casallas/Rodrigo Fernandez
4) Stilo
5) 1979(Colombia)
6) gray
285
2),3) Hans Weber
4) Rolf Jller Genf
5) 1975(Switzerland)
6) gray/blue→M4
286 1) drugstore
2) Joe Selame

Building
5) 1982(Japan)
6) yellow/black
345 1) design company
2) Yoichi Sugamura
3) Michiko Sugamura
4) Moirés
5) 1982(Japan)
6) black/red
346 1) shop lighting(contest)
2) Nobuyuki Hagiwara/Hiroshi
Matsuda
3) Fumio Koyoda
4) Matsushita Electric Works
5) 1982(Japan)
347 1) family restaurant
3) Helmut Schmidt
4) Sun Valley
5) 1981(Japan)
6) gradation from red to orange
348 1) automobile
2),3) Armin Vogt
4) Fiat Italia
5) 1967(Switzerland)
6) Pantone 293
349 1) restaurant, pub
2),3) Shintaro Ajioka
4) Miami
5) 1981(Japan)
350 1) automobile
2),3) Armin Vogt
4) Fiat Italia
5) 1967(Switzerland)
6) Pantone 116
351 1) record
2) Carlos Rolando
3) Jose Carlos Rodriguez
4) Sal Común
5) 1975(Spain)
6) black/white
352 1) magazine
2) Kenzo Nakagawa
3) Hiroyasu Nobuyama/
Satoshi Morikami
4) Daily Industry Newspaper Inc.
5) 1982(Japan)
353 1) theatre
2) David Lock
3) Glenn Tutssel
4) Strarford East Company
5) 1977(England)
6) deep red
354 1) selling with a premium
2) Osamu Ogawa
3) Hajime Fujii
4) Ogawa Design Office
5) 1981(Japan)
355 1) camping
2),3) Alfredo de Santis
4) Lignano Pineta Ltd.
5) 1979(Italy)
356 1) photography studio
3) Kenji Kaneko
4) Sky Box
5) 1981(Japan)
357 1) design office
2),3) Yasumasa Oka
4) Design Office Milky Way
5) 1975(Japan)
358 1) photography studio
2),3) Hajime Yoshimura
4) Life Studio
5) 1980(Japan)
359 1) articles of furniture
(brand)

2) Teruo Fujishige
3) Teruo Fujishige/Yoji
Hayakawa
4) Maruni Carpentry
5) 1977(Japan)
360 1) furniture company
(brand)
2) Shigeo Katsuoka
3) Hiroshi Asami
4) Maruichi Selling
5) 1981(Japan)
361 1) department store
(jewelry exhibition)
3) Helmut Schmidt
4) Takashimaya
5) 1981(Japan)
6) gold
362 1) record label
2) Ikko Tanaka
3) Ikko Tanaka/Toshine
Ishihama
4) Phonogram
5) 1980(Japan)
363 1) construction
(foundation work)
2),3) PVDI
4) Franki
5) 1973(Brazil)
364 1) magazine
2) Shigo Yamaguchi
3) Hisako Nagano
4) Swing Journal Co.,Ltd.
5) 1983(Japan)
365 1) sport(club)
2),3) Scott Engen
4) Sports AM
5) 1983(USA)
6) black/red(PMS 032)
366 1) uniform
2),3) Kazuo Kishimoto
4) Baseball Team(Team Izumi)
5) 1979(Japan)
367 1) automobile parts
2),3) Moriyoshi Iijima
4) Lears
5) 1978(Japan)
368 1) medical
2) Alfonso Capetillo Ponce
3) Vicente Guerrero
4) Lubric Adhitiva, S.A.
5) 1974(Mexico)
6) black/red/blue
369 1) camera(campaign for
sequence photographs)
2),3) Yasaburo Kuwayama
4) Olympus Optical Industry
5) 1980(Japan)
370 1) catering car
2) Kotaro Kurosaki/Kenzo
Nakagawa
3) Kenzo Nakagawa/Sumiko
Tsutani
4) Nippon Vending
5) 1982(Japan)
371 1) maker of electric
appliances
2),3) Minoru Takahashi
4) Sony
5) 1982(Japan)
372 1) lighting equipment
2),3) Minoru Takahashi
4) Ushio Spax
5) 1979(Japan)
373
3) Jan Hollender

4) Agropol
5) 1983(Poland)
374 1) computer
2),3) Bruce D. Zahor
4) Apro Systems Inc.
5) 1982(USA)
375 1) publication
2),3) Christor Gassner
4) Öko Test Magazine
5) 1983(West Germany)
6) black/red→C48
376 1) electronic industry
2),3) Dominik Burckhardt
4) Mediator
5) 1981(Switzerland)
6) black
377 1) engineering(protection
against heat)
2),3) Irmgaid Sonner
4) Isomura Co.,Ltd.
5) 1980(West Germany)
6) black/red/blue
378 1) automobile parts(brand)
2),3) Sogen Oonishi
4) Jilba Racing Sales
5) 1982(Japan)
6) golden red(M100 + Y100)
379 1) multi-business
2) João Carlos Cauduro/
Ludovico Antonio Martino
4) Siderúrgica Nossa Senhora
da Aparecida e Coligadas
5) 1980(Brazil)
380 1) multi-business
2) João Carlos Cauduro/
Ludovico Antonio Martino
4) Siderúrgica Nossa Senhora
da Aparecida e Coligadas
5) 1980(Brazil)
381 1) multi-business
2) João Carlos Cauduro/
Ludovico Antonio Martino
4) Siderúrgica Nossa Senhora
da Aparecida e Coligadas
5) 1972(Brazil)
382 1) petroleum company
3) Aloisio Magalhães/
Rodrigues Rafael/Roberto Lanari
4) Petróleo Brasileiro
5) 1970(Brazil)
383 1) multi-business
2) João Carlos Cauduro/
Ludovico Antonio Martino
4) Corporação Bonfiglioli
5) 1981(Brazil)
384 1) advertisement
2),3) Kimito Oohashira
4) Nihon Sign
5) 1981(Japan)
385 1) chemistry
2),3) Kazutoshi Uemoto/Kozo
Higashihara
4) Yamato Chemical Industry
5) 1983(Japan)
386 1) social security
2) João Carlos Cauduro/
Ludovico Antonio Martino
4) Fundação FAELBA
5) 1980(Brazil)
387 1) electrical authority
2) João Carlos Cauduro/
Ludovico Antonio Martino
4) CPFL
5) 1978(Brazil)
388 1) banking

2) João Carlos Cauduro/
Ludovico Antonio Martino
4) Banco do Estado de São
Paulo SA
5) 1975(Brazil)
389 1) building
2) João Carlos Cauduro/
Ludovico Antonio Martino
4) Schahim Cury Engenharia
Co.,Ltd.
5) 1976(Brazil)
390 1) industry
2) João Carlos Cauduro/
Ludovico Antonio Martino
4) Morlan
5) 1978(Brazil)
391 1) commerce
2),3) Irmgaid Sonner
4) Sonnen-Herzog
5) 1979(West Germany)
6) red
392 1) precision measuring
instruments(manufacturer)
2),3) Koichi Yamada
4) Tokyo Seimitsu
5) 1977(Japan)
393 1) cigarette
2),3) Oanh Pham-Phu
4) Philip Morris
5) 1980(West Germany)
394
3) Jan Hollander
4) Megat
5) 1983(Poland)
395 1) finance
3) Rodrigues Rafael/Nair
Iannibelli
4) London Multiplic S.A.
5) (Brazil)
6) green
396 1) electrical authority
2) João Carlos Cauduro/
Ludovico Antonio Martino
4) Celetramazon
5) 1980(Brazil)
397 1) transportation
2) Joe Selame
3) Selame Design Group
4) Hemingway Transport Co.
5) 1973(USA)
6) deep red
398 1) movie(production)
2),3) Conrad E. Angone
4) Ukopia Productions
5) 1972(USA)
6) black
399
2) Stankowski & Duschek
3) Anton Stankowdki
4) Schierling
5) 1976(West Germany)
400
2) Stankowski & Duschek
3) Anton Stankowski
4) Schaeffer Scovill
5) 1975-82(West Germany)
401 1) heat exchangers
(manufacturer)
2) Ove Engstrom
3) Ove Engstrom/Torgny
Gustavsson
4) ELGE
5) 1978(Sweden)
6) red/black/green
402 1) department store

2),3) Allan W. Miller
4) Tourism Committee of City of Tijuana
5) 1976(USA)
6) magenta
460 1) restaurant
2) Maurizio Milani／Armando Milani
3) Maurizio Milani
4) Fiona
5) 1979(Italy)
461 1) microcomputer magazine
2),3) Makoto Yoshida
4) Kosaido Publishing
5) 1978(Japan)
6) golden red(M100 + Y100)
462 1) market research, consulting
2),3) Masatoshi Shimokawa
4) Blobal Link(Los Angeles)
5) 1975(Japan)
6) blue
463 1) clothing(resort wear)
3) Shigetoshi Shibata
4) Yoshinoto
5) 1978(Japan)
464 1) building
2) Kazuo Maekawa
3) shigo Yamaguchi
4) Matsushita Investment and Development
5) 1983(Japan)
6) green(DIC 175)
465 1) restaurant
2) Shigeru Sato
4) Bamboo
5) 1978(Japan)
6) green
466 1) design company
2) Tadashi Ishikawa
3) Hideko Sakato
4) Dokko Research Institute of Design
5) 1975(Japan)
467 1) automobile(showroom)
2),3) Ken'ichi Kaneko
4) Gunma Toyopet(Car Pit)
5) 1983(Japan)
468
2),3) Pietro Galli
4) Rock Soil
5) 1979(Italy)
6) black
469 1) consultant(nutrition)
2) Don Davis Design
3) Don Davis
4) New Life Nutrition Consultants
5) 1983(USA)
6) green／copper
470 1) record
2),3) Jorge Sposari
4) Compañia Grabadora Clave
5) 1974(Argentina)
471
3) Paul Ibou
4) Libelle Rosita
5) 1970(Belgium)
472 1) sound equipment facilities(manufacturer)
2) Sudarshan Dheer
3) Pravin Sevak
4) Multivision
5) 1979(India)

6) gray
473 1) entertainment(exhibition)
2),3) Shunji Kanda
4) Aron Chemical Synthesis
5) 1980(Japan)
6) blue／M100 + C100
474 1) shopping center
2),3) Teruo Fujishige
4) Pair City Mihara
5) 1981(Japan)
475 1) title of a magazine article
2),3) Shigo Yamaguchi
4) Swing Journal Co.,Ltd.
5) 1981(Japan)
476 1) guidebook title
3) Yasumasa Oka
4) Osaka Design Academy
5) 1977(Japan)
477 1) pub
3) Shinji Arakawa
3) Kazunari Nishida
4) Cat's Cradle
5) 1982(Japan)
478 1) boutique
3) Yoshikatsu Tami
4) More
5) 1982(Japan)
479 1) beauty salon
2),3) Takeshi Ootaka
4) Mode Beauty Salon
5) 1974(Japan)
480 1) cosmetic
2) Shigehiko Takizawa
3) Ikuo Masubuchi
4) Japan Charmqueen
5) 1980(Japan)
481 1) wine(label)
2),3) Yasaburo Kuwayama
4) Ushiki Domestic and Foreign Patent Office
5) 1975(Japan)
482 1) title of a trade publication
3) Kazunari Nishida
4) Japan Typography Association
5) 1980(Japan)
483 1) office furniture
3) Marcello d'Andrea
4) Spazio
5) 1977(Italy)
6) black／white
484 1) department store (entertainment)
2) Studio Tamu
3) Tadasu Fukano
4) Seibu Department Store
5) 1974(Japan)
485 1) clothing
2),3) Guillermo González Ruiz
4) Roland Cotton
5) 1983(Argentina)
6) black
486 1) committee(sports)
3) Velizar Petrov
4) Committee for Youth and Sports
5) 1974(Bulgaria)
487 1) resort
2),3) Yusaku Kamekura
4) Appi Comprehensive Development
5) 1982(Japan)
488 1) textile(manufacturer)

2) Shigeru Shimooka
3) Masanobu Watanabe
4) Avelco
5) 1981(Japan)
489 1) jewel shop
2),3) Kazunari Nishida
4) Jewel Shima
5) 1973(Japan)
490 1) measuring instrument of three-dimensional coordinates
2),3) Koichi Yamada
4) Tokyo Seimitsu
5) 1978(Japan)
491 1) automobile
2),3) Shin Matsunaga
4) Toyo Industry
5) 1972(Japan)
492 1) trust
2),3) Michael Baviera
4) Real Estate Trust Company
5) 1974(Switzerland)
6) black
493 1) telephone (manufacturer)
3) Velizar Petrov
4) Nvactиka
5) 1982(Bulgaria)
494 1) center for the arts
2),3) Burton Kramer
4) St. Lawrence Center
5) 1983(Canada)
6) gold／silver → C40,41
495 1) elevator industry
2),3) PVDI
4) Indústria de Elevadores Apolo
5) 1970(Brazil)
496 1) woodwork (manufacturer)
3) Ricardo Blanco
4) Carpintería Mecanica Latina
5) 1971(Argentina)
6) brown
497
2),3) Stuart Winnard
4) Beauty Bronze
5) 1982(Great Britain)
6) black
498
2),3) PVDI
4) Sicpa
5) 1971(Brazil)
499 1) manufacturing
2),3) Stephan Kantscheff
4) Mineral Souvenir
5) (Bulgaria)
500 1) hotel
2) Lew Lehrman
3) Debbie Kossoff
4) Puerto Rico Hyatt Hotel
5) 1976(USA)
501 1) machine(manufacturer)
2),3) Gavin Healey
4) Honeywell Europe
5) 1983(England)
6) red → C35
502 1) boutique
2),3) Hiromi Nagano
4) Musique
5) 1972(Japan)
503 1) radio station
2) Ray Engle
3) Jerome Jensik
4) KFI 640
5) 1972(USA)

6) brown
504 1) food
2),3) Jorge Canales
4) Productos Alianza
5) 1978(Mexico)
6) blue(Pantone 285)
505 1) committee(tourism)
2),3) Allan W. Miller
4) Tourism Committee of City of Tocate
5) 1978(USA)
6) orange
506 1) construction, building design
2),3) Gavin Healey
4) The Lesser Group
5) 1970(England)
6) blue → C46, M2
507 1) color television
2),3) Shigeo Komori
4) NEC Home Electronics
5) 1982(Japan)
508 1) dress shop
3) Marcello d' Andrea
4) City Club
5) 1974(Italy)
6) black／white
509
2),3) Michael Baviera
4) Michael Baviera
5) 1970(Switzerland)
6) black
510 1) teahouse
2),3) Takeo Nakahara
4) Marutama
5) 1978(Japan)
511 1) ecological defense
2),3) Massimo Dradi
4) ECODECO
5) 1970(Italy)
6) black
512 1) restaurant with live jazz
2),3) Ken'ichi Hirose
4) Ballantine's 2
5) 1981(Japan)
513 1) publishing house
3) Marcello d'Andrea
4) AGORA
5) 1980(Italy)
6) black／white
514 1) textile industry
3) Marcello d'Andrea
4) MTP
5) 1975(Italy)
515 1) French confectionery shop
2),3) Ken'ichi Hirose
4) Bonne Chere
5) 1977(Japan)
516 1) chemical industry
3) István Szekeres
4) Tiszai Vegyi Kombinát
5) 1974(Hungary)
6) yellowish brown
517
3) Yoshimitsu Kato
4) Bentom
5) 1982(Japan)
518 1) automobile parts (aluminum wheel)
2) Moriyoshi Iijima
3) Moriyoshi Iijima／Masazumi Ainoya
4) Seiwa
5) 1981(Japan)

3) Milton Glaser/George Leavitt
4) Amall Leasures & Bear Necessities/George Lang Corp.
5) 1978(USA)
6) brown/white
577 1) event shop(tentative plan)
2),3) Yasuhiko Shibukawa
5) 1982(Japan)
578 1) transportation
2),3) Jorge Canales
4) Transportes C.S.A.
5) 1979(Mexico)
6) red
579
3) Daphne Duijvelshoff
4) Katan BV
5) 1979(Netherlands)
6) blue/black
580 1) flooring industry
3) A. G. Schillemans
4) Nierstrasz Vloeren BV
5) 1979(Netherlands)
6) dark brown
581
3) Jan Hollender
4) Pianka
5) 1983(Poland)
582 1) New Year's card
3) Toshiaki Takahashi
4) Toshiaki Takahashi
5) 1982(Japan)
583 1) food
2),3) Takeshi Ootaka
4) Nissin Food Products
5) 1982(Japan)
584 1) food(brand)
2),3) Takeshi Ootaka
4) Nissn Foods Products
5) 1983(Japan)
585 1) fast food
2),3) David Leigh(Murtha, De Sola, Finsilver, Fiore, Inc.)
4) Speakeasy Pizza
5) 1981(USA)
6) red/black
586 1) roller coaster
2) Toshihiko Matsuo
3) Katsuichi Ito
4) Yokohama Dream Land
5) 1980(Japan)
587 1) correspondence course
3) Kaoru Iida
4) Scande Furniture Institute
5) 1977(Japan)
588 1) construction
2),3) Tony Forster
4) Zenex Partnership Ltd.
5) 1981(England)
6) gray
589 1) company name
2),3) Osamu Furumura
4) Wings
5) 1981(Japan)
590
2) Tadashi Ishikawa
3) Hideko Sakato
4) Aoki Giken Development
5) 1974(Japan)
591 1) entertainment(private exhibition)
2),3) Masayuki Yano
4) Sunako Hata
5) 1979(Japan)
592 1) record title

2),3) Masayuki Yano
4) Epic/Sony
5) 1979(Japan)
593 1) discoteque
2),3) Tadasu Fukano
4) Naeba Prince Hotel
5) 1973(Japan)
594 1) stationery
2),3) Ernesto Lehfeld
4) Ernesto Lehfeld
5) 1973(Mexico)
6) black
595 1) coffee shop
2),3) Milton Glaser
4) Inhilco
5) 1977(USA)
6) brown/white
596 1) guidebook title
3) Yasumasa Oka
4) Osaka Design Academy
5) 1980(Japan)
597 1) title of a magazine article
2),3) Shigo Yamaguchi
4) Swing Journal Co.,Ltd.
5) 1983(Japan)
598 1) book title
2),3) Yasumasa Oka
4) CBS Sony Publishing
5) 1981(Japan)
599 1) guidebook title
3) Yasumasa Oka
4) Osaka Design Academy
5) 1978(Japan)
600 1) acoustics company (catalogue)
2) Toshiyasu Nanbu
3) Yasumasa Yamamoto
4) Yasuda Construction
5) 1982(Japan)
601 1) tearoom, snack bar
2) Shunji Niinomi
3) Tetsuharu Mabuchi
4) Bianco
5) 1976(Japan)
602 1) restaurant
3) Assen Ivanov
4) Rubin
5) 1983(Bulgaria)
603 1) pub and restaurant
3) Shigo Yamaguchi
4) Half Note
5) 1979(Japan)
604 1) pamphlet
2) Nobuyuki Nagaoka
3) Masahiro Toki
4) NEC Corporation Environmental Engineering
5) 1983(Japan)
605 1) restaurant
2),3) Tsutomu Shimoyama
4) Hatsushima
5) 1981(Japan)
606 1) restaurant
3) Yoneo Jinbo
4) Robata
5) 1975(Japan)
607 1) publishing
2),3) Jagdish Chavda
4) Bharati Publications Inc.
5) (USA)
608 1) apparatus a fish-luring light(manufacturer)
2),3) Masaaki Fukuda
4) North Japan Fishery
5) 1983(Japan)

609 1) private symbol(graphic designer)
2),3) Steve Allen
4) Steve Allen
5) 1981(USA)
6) multicolor
610 1) antique shop
2),3) Carlos Rolando
4) Susana Koruer
5) 1979(Spain)
6) black/gold
611 1) machine(selling)
2),3) Tom Lewis
4) Al's Machine Shop
5) 1977(USA)
612
2),3) Thomas J. Ambrosino
4) Custom Collision
5) 1983(USA)
6) black/white
613 1) calendar(cover)
2),3) Masahiro Abe
4) Abe Design-R.
5) 1979(Japan)
614 1) map scanning systems
2),3) Leif F. Anisdahl
4) Sysscan A.S.
5) 1982(Norway)
6) blue
615 1) construction
2),3) Eduardo A. Cánovas
4) Del Sol S.A.
5) 1979(Argentina)
6) ochre
616 1) development
2),3) Gavin Healey
4) British Urban Development Services Unit
5) 1977(England)
6) light blue
617 1) real estate
2),3) Marty Neumeier
4) West Pac Shelter Corp.
5) 1979(USA)
6) blue/green
618 1) construction
3) Matjaž Bertonceli
4) Giposs
5) 1978(Yugoslavia)
6) black/green
619 1) cement
2),3) PVDI
4) Grupo Paraiso
5) 1971(Brazil)
620 1) furniture
2),3) Takenobu Igarashi
4) Build
5) 1982(Japan)
621 1) construction
2),3) Gustavo Gomez-Casallas
4) Corinvia-Consorcio
5) 1977(Columbia)
6) blue(cobalt)
622 1) restaurant
2),3) Kazuo Tajima
4) Eve
5) 1976(Japan)
623 1) paper merchant
2),3) Carl Christensen
4) Boman Papir
5) 1978(Norway)
624 1) catalogue
2),3) Toshiyasu Nanbu
4) Daiko Electric Works
5) 1971(Japan)

625 1) student encyclopedia(Solaris)
2) Kazutoshi Furihata
3) Makoto Yoshida/Honami Morita
4) Gakken Co.,Ltd.
5) 1983(Japan)
6) rainbow colors
626 1) turbo automobile
2),3) The Design Department of the Isuzu Automobile Industry
4) The Isuzu Automobile Industry
5) 1982(Japan)
6) dark gray/dark green/warm silver/dark blue/warm gray
627 1) interior design (scheme, execution)
2),3) Shigeo Katsuoka
4) Enoch
5) 1975(Japan)
6) orange(DIC 119)
628 1) boutique
2) Massimo Dradi
3) Aldo Travagliati
4) Krisma
5) 1982(Italy)
6) black/orange/yellow
629 1) fashion designer
3) Kaoru Iida
4) Can Group
5) 1976(Japan)
630 1) entertainment
2) Kuniharu Masubuchi
3) Ikuo Masubuchi
4) Mikimoto
5) 1977(Japan)
631 1) exhibition
2) John Constable
3) Victor Dicristo
4) Illustrators & Designers
5) 1978(USA)
6) black
632
2) Renato Gomes
3) Angela Ribeiro
4) Newsplan
5) 1980(Brazil)
6) red
633 1) electronic components
3) A. G. Schillemans
4) Amroh BV
5) 1974(Netherlands)
6) orange
634 1) artist
2),3) Masayuki Yano
4) Discomate Record
5) 1980(Japan)
635 1) postal card
2),3) Koji Nagai
4) Can
5) 1981(Japan)
636 1) broadcasting station
2),3) Yoshihiro Yoshida
4) Nippon Broadcasting
5) 1983(Japan)
637 1) snack bar and tea room
2),3) Shuji Torigoe
4) Restaurant Tokyu
5) 1975(Japan)
638 1) campaign
2),3) Masayuki Yano
4) CBS Sony

5) 1983(Japan)
698 1) lithograph
2),3) Rey R. Dacosta
4) Altosca
5) 1981(Venezuela)
6) blue
699 1) airline
2) Saul Bass
3) Saul Bass/Herb Yager Associates
4) United Airlines
5) 1974(USA)
6) black
700 1) automobile
2) So Takano
3) Katsuichi Ito
4) Isuzu Automobile
5) 1982(Japan)
701 1) precision plastic products(manufacture, selling)
2),3) Ken'ichi Hirose
4) Daiichi Precision Machinery Industry
5) 1981(Japan)
6) blue
702 1) electric appliance
2),3) Hiroshi Toida
4) Matsunaga Workshop
5) 1982(Japan)
703 1) display company
2),3) Ken'ichi Hirose
4) Murayama
5) 1982(Japan)
6) blue/green
704 1) sheet metal
3) Kazuharu Fujii
4) Nimura Sheet Metal Industry
5) 1981(Japan)
705 1) electronic industry
2),3) Ray Engle
4) International Electric Research Corporation
5) 1971(USA)
6) black
706
2) Gunter Mohr
3) Gary Ball
4) Skookum, Inc.
5) 1972(USA)
6) blue
707 1) duplicator
2),3) Yasaburo Kuwayama
4) Olympus Optical Industry
5) 1979(Japan)
6) blue/black/white
708 1) electronics
2) Peter Christensen
3) Marc Burkhalter
4) Gretag Inc.
5) 1982(Switzerland)
6) blue
709 1) camera
2) Takeya Mitani/Yasaburo Kuwayama
3) Yasaburo Kuwayama/Atsushi Ichihashi
4) Olympus Optical Industry
5) 1983(Japan)
710 1) department store with large scale selling of home
2) Ichiro Tatsumi
3) Takeo Sugaya
4) Seidensha
5) 1981(Japan)
6) dark blue(DIC 183)

711 1) medicine(selling)
2) Joe Vera
3) Joe Vera/Francisco Tellez
4) Farmax
5) 1974(Mexico)
6) blue
712 1) canning
2),3) Koichi Watanabe
4) Hotei Canning
5) 1982(Japan)
713 1) beverage (manufacturer)
3) G. Edwards
4) Balseca
5) 1978(Mexico)
6) blue
714
2) Alfonso Capetillo Ponce
3) Ricardo Salas
4) Tubos de Acero de Mexico
5) 1980(Mexico)
6) gray
715 1) balloon lovers' society
2),3) Yukio Kanise
4) Balloon
5) 1978(Japan)
716 1) optical industry
2),3) Helfried Hagenberg
4) NiGuRa
5) 1970(West Germany)
6) red
717 1) atomic industry
2),3) Tokyo Shibaura Denki
4) Nihon Genshiryoku Jigyo Co.,Ltd.
5) 1977(Japan)
718 1) real estate
3) Tsuyokatsu Kudo
4) Kakoh Co.,Ltd.
5) 1979(Japan)
719 1) management consultant
2) Akira Hirata
3) Akira Hirata/Koji Mori
4) Nihon LCA Co.,Ltd.
5) 1983(Japan)
6) green(Pantone 354)/gray(Pantone 404)
720 1) illuminator manufacturer
2),3) Minoru Takahashi
4) Ushio Spax
5) 1979(Japan)
721 1) industrial vehicles
3) Paolo De Robertis/Carlo Malerba/Giorgio Tramontini
4) IVECO
5) 1979(Italy)
6) blue
722 1) food company
2) John DiGianni
3) Gianninoto Associates, Inc.
4) Thomas J. Lipton, Inc.
5) 1983(USA)
6) red
723 1) office machines
2) Itoshoji/Yoshihiro Kishimoto
3) Yoshihiro Kishimoto
4) Itoshoji
5) 1983(Japan)
6) blue/green
724
2) Carlo Malerba
3) Carlo Malerba/Franco Assom

4) Walserel
5) 1980(Italy)
6) green
725 1) bank
2),3) Jorge Canales
4) Banco Nacional Pesquero y Portuario S.A.
5) 1981(Mexico)
6) blue/green
726
2) Monica Morales
3) Carmen Cordela
4) Plantaciones Tropicales
5) 1982(Mexico)
6) green(Pantone 363/553)
727 1) exhibition
3) Fumio Koyoda
4) Osaka Graphic Association
5) 1983(Japan)
728 1) sportswear
2),3) Fumio Koyoda
4) Kosugi Sangyo Co.,Ltd.
5) 1979(Japan)
729 1) automobile
2) Isamu Abe
3) Shigo Yamaguchi
4) Nissan
5) 1978(Japan)
730 1) automobile
2) Yasuo Suzuki
3) Shigo Yamaguchi
4) Toyota
5) 1977(Japan)
731 1) leather goods
2),3) Kuniharu Masubuchi
4) Yamaura Senkaku Co.,Ltd.
5) 1980(Japan)
732 1) printing
2),3) Yukihisa Takakita
4) Totani Insatsho
5) 1979(Japan)
733 1) manufacturer of refrigerators
2),3) Walter Hergenröther
4) ACFIS
5) 1973(Italy)
6) blue/light turquoise
734 1) manufacturer of refrigeration
2),3) Walter Hergenröther
4) NEMO Europe
5) 1977(Italy)
6) prussian blue/green turquoise
735 1) studio
2),3) Ikko Tanaka
4) Studio Ebis
5) 1983(Japan)
736 1) brand of sport shoes
2) Iwao Hosoya
3) Tadasu Fukano
4) Kokoku Kagakogyo
5) 1977(Japan)
737 1) campaign
2),3) Takeshi Otaka
4) Nissin Food Products Co.,Ltd.
5) 1983(Japan)
738 1) restaurant
2),3) Minoru Takahashi
4) Osada Pacific
5) 1983(Japan)
739 1) title of magazine
3) Shin Matsunaga/Osamu Furuta
4) Diamond Co.,Ltd.
5) 1982(Japan)

740 1) graphics/products/environmental design
2),3) George Delany
4) Aalpha Communications Group
5) 1983(USA)
6) black/violet
741 1) computer
2),3) Chermayeff & Geismar Associates
4) Adage, Inc.
5) (USA)
6) green
742 1) business equipment
2),3) Chermayeff & Geismar Associates
4) Uarco Inc.
5) (USA)
6) black
743 1) plastics manufacturer
2),3) Othmar Motter
4) ALPLA
5) 1982(Austria)
6) black/white
744 1) electric shaver
3) Helmut Schmidt
4) Sanyo Electric Co.,Ltd.
5) 1977(Japan)
745 1) bank
3) Wim Crouwel
4) Rabo Bank
5) 1973(Netherlands)
6) blue(Pantone 293C)
746 1) metal industry
3) A.G. Schillemans
4) Daaldelop
5) 1978(Netherlands)
6) dark blue/light blue
747 1) transport(railway)
2),3) Stephan Kantscheff
4) Bulgarian State Railway
5) 1972(Bulgaria)
748 1) service store
2) Ryosuke Matsuki
4) Tsuruya Hyakkaten
5) 1980(Japan)
749
2),3) Heinz Waibl
4) Skema Arredamenti
5) 1982(Italy)
750 1) fair and store construction
2),3) Oanh Pham-Phu
4) F. Burger
5) 1970(West Germany)
6) gray silver
751 1) publication
2),3) Shigo Yamaguchi
4) Swing Jorunal
5) 1983(Japan)
752 1) pottery industry
2),3) Akira Hirata
4) Ito Yogyo Co.,Ltd.
5) 1970(Japan)
753 1) hotel
3) Yukinori Yamashita
4) Unzen Park Hotel
5) 1970(Japan)
6) cobalt blue/scarlet
754
2),3) Jan Hollender
4) Megadex
5) 1983(Poland)
755 1) film production
3) Marcello d'Andrea

2) Joe Selame
3) Selame Design Group
4) Sterilite Plastics Inc.
5) 1970(USA)
6) black／magenta
818
2),3) Steve Shelden
4) Hubert・Saws
5) 1982(USA)
6) white／dark blue
819
2) Ricardo Salas
3) Javier De Leon
4) Tintas Sanchez, S.A.
5) 1981(Mexico)
6) gray／black
820 1) restaurant
2),3) Juan Ignacio Gomez
4) Restaurante Piscis
5) 1983(Mexico)
6) blue(Pantone 298)
821
2) C. Y. Sneider
3) Bob Schoelkopf
4) Hexcel
5) 1972(USA)
6) black
822 1) distributor of heavy equipment
2),3) Rey R. Dacosta
4) Decsa
5) 1973(Venezuela)
6) red
823 1) crane rental
2),3) Rey R. Dacosta
4) Gruas Guanipa
5) 1982(Venezuela)
6) black
824 1) food manufacturer
3) Yasumasa Oka
4) My Thatcher's
5) 1979(Japan)
6) red
825 1) fast food
3) Yasumasa Oka
4) My Thatcher's
5) 1979(Japan)
6) red
826 1) title of magazine
2) Masato Kumazawa
3) Hiroshi Iseya
4) Kyodo Tsushin Co.,Ltd.
5) 1981(Japan)
827 1) title of magazine
2),3) Yoshihiro Yoshida
4) Nihon Research Center
5) 1973(Japan)
828 1) manufacturer of car stereos
2) Tsuyoshi Fukuda
3) Shigo Yamaguchi
4) Alpine
5) 1979(Japan)
829 1) publishing
3) Miloš Ćirić
4) Danas
5) 1983(Yugoslavia)
830 1) optical apparatus
2),3) Kaoru Iida
4) Sigma
5) 1983(Japan)
831 1) boutique
2) Yasaburo Kuwayama
3) Takero Shiodera
4) Square

5) 1983(Japan)
832 1) manufacturer of medical instruments
2),3) Masaaki Fukuda
4) Tanaka Sangyo Co.,Ltd.
5) 1980(Japan)
833 1) manufacturer of analyzing apparatus and vacuum apparatus
2) Koichi Mizuno
3) Masatoshi Iwamoto
4) Nichiden Anelva Corporation
5) 1978(Japan)
6) green
834 1) copiers
3) Tsuneo Shimada
4) NEC Corporation
5) 1978(Japan)
835 1) sportswear
2) Kenji Shigematsu
3) Yoko Satomi
4) Shimoguchi
5) 1983(Japan)
6) blue
836 1) audio apparatus
2) Shigeru Shimooka
3) Toyohiko Sugimoto
4) Nihon Marantzu, Inc.
5) 1983(Japan)
837
2),3) Ken'ichi Hirose
4) Sundelta, Inc.
5) 1981(Japan)
838 1) photo film
3) Shin Matsunaga／Osamu Furuta
4) Konishi Roku Shashin -kogyo
5) 1983(Japan)
839 1) commercial firm
2) Tadashi Ishikawa
3) Hideko Sakato
4) Rising Sun
5) 1978(Japan)
840 1) paper manufacturing company
2),3) Madeleine Bujatti
4) Leykam
5) 1982(Austria)
6) black／blue
841 1) dairy products
2),3) Tadasu Fukano
4) Morinaga Nyugyo
5) 1981(Japan)
842 1) shop
2),3) Yusaku Kamekura
4) Livina Yamagiwa
5) 1983(Japan)
6) blue／blue green／yellow／light brown
843 1) supermarket
2) Yasaburo Kuwayama
3) Hiroshi Iseya
4) Super Shimaya
5) 1976(Japan)
844
2),3) Tadasu Fukano
4) Nihon Kokan
5) 1974(Japan)
845 1) furniture
2),3) Tadasu Fukano
4) Linear Japan
5) 1974(Japan)
846
2),3) Milton Glaser

4) Grand Union Company
5) 1979(USA)
6) black／red
847
2),3) Angelo Sganzerla
4) Laurens-Milano
5) 1982(Italy)
6) black
848 1) highway construction company
2),3) Nicolay Pecareff
4) Ingstroi
5) 1982(Bulgaria)
6) black／yellow
849
3) Velizar Petrov
4) Plant Madara
5) 1970(Bulgaria)
6) red
850 1) trading
2) Felix Beltran
3) Monica Reyes
4) Interexport, S.A.
5) 1983(Mexico)
6) brown
851 1) color television
2) Shn'ichi Horiuchi
3) Yuji Baba
4) NEC Home Electronics
5) 1983(Japan)
852
2) Felix Beltran
3) Teresa Echartea
4) Mecanoflex
5) 1983(Mexico)
6) deep gray
853 1) laser disc system
2) Hiroshi Fujiwara
3) Kazunari Nishida
4) Pioneer Electronic Corporation
5) 1981(Japan)
854 1) hotel
2) Carmen Cordela
3) Juan Ignacio Gomez
4) Promotera Hotelera Misión
5) 1982(Mexico)
6) brown(Pantone 154)
855 1) cosmetics
2),3) Shigeo Katsuoka
4) Doctor Sakurai Keshohin Co.
5) 1982(Japan)
856 1) electrical promotion
2),3) Tokyo Shibaura Denki
4) Tokyo Shibaura Denki
5) 1983(Japan)
6) red／black
857
2),3) Silvio Coppola
4) Cilsa
5) 1968(Italy)
858 1) French restaurant
2),3) Takenobu Igarashi
4) Restaurant Escargot
5) 1972(Japan)
859 1) television production company
2),3) Eita Shinohara
4) JASC Inc.
5) 1976(Japan)
860 1) boutique
2),3) Takenobu Igarashi
4) Boutique la Ronde
5) 1974(Japan)
861 1) adhesive

3) Yutaka Sato
4) Fukushin Shoji
5) 1980(Japan)
862 1) clothing manufacturer
3) Stephan Kantscheff
4) Denitza Haskobo
5) 1982(Bulgaria)
863 1) planning magazine
2),3) Takeo Nakahara
4) Matsushita Electric Co.,Ltd.
5) 1983(Japan)
864 1) association(advertising)
2),3) Tadasu Fukano
4) Organization of Ad-creative Corporations
5) 1974(Japan)
865 1) fashion(Grace Group)
2) Koichi Nakai
3) Ichiro Nakai／Tetsuo Hiro／Tetsuo Togasawa
4) Grace
5) 1982(Japan)
6) wine color
866 1) window cleaners
2),3) Harumasa Misaki
4) Tokyo BM Tops Co.,Ltd.
5) 1980(Japan)
867 1) car dealer
2) Osamu Kayaba
3) Kenji Yamashita
4) Toyota Motor
5) 1980(Japan)
6) red／dark blue
868 1) clothing
2),3) Shuji Torigoe
4) Tokyu Store
5) 1970(Japan)
869 1) shoe manufacturer
2) Nobuyoshi Nakanishi
3) Yoshio Hirano
4) Achilles Corporation Inc.
5) 1980(Japan)
6) pastel color／black
870 1) title of magazine
3) Shin Matsunaga
4) Shueisha
5) 1982(Japan)
871 1) lighting
2),3) Minoru Takahashi
4) Ushio Denki
5) 1978(Japan)
872 1) travel agency
2),3) Tadasu Fukano
4) Nissan Air Service Co.,Ltd.
5) 1981(Japan)
873 1) sport(golf course)
2) Yasaburo Kuwayama
3) Minoru Kamono
4) Togoku-sogyo
5) 1976(Japan)
874 1) association(finish work)
2) Yasaburo Kuwayama
3) Yasaburo Kuwayama／Muneo Mizumori
4) Nihon Finish Work Kyokai
5) 1976(Japan)
875 1) foods producer
2) Gary Ball
3) Dave Baca
4) Pik・Nik Foods, Inc.
5) 1978(USA)
6) black
876 1) travel agency
3) Yasunori Satake
4) Shikoku Travel Service, Inc.

4) Victory Van Lines Inc.
5) (USA)
935 1) publisher
3) Adrian Frutiger
4) Hallwag
5) 1979(France)
6) black
936 1) publisher
2),3) Jorge Sposari
4) Editorial America Norildis
Editores S.A.
5) 1975(Argentina)
937 1) resort wear
2) Yoriya Ueda
3) Kunihiro Adachi
4) Seibu Dept. Stores
5) 1983(Japan)
938 1) candle shop
2),3) Harry Murphy
4) Candles To Burn
5) 1969(USA)
6) black/white
939 1) lounge
2),3) Tadasu Fukano
4) Naeba Prince Hotel
5) 1973(Japan)
940 1) rivet manufacturer
2),3) Manfred Korten
4) König Nietefabrik
5) 1977(West Germany)
6) black
941 1) interior planner
2),3) Georg Staehelin
4) WB Projekt AG
5) 1981(Switzerland)
6) black/red
942 1) corn refinery
2),3) Eduardo A. Canovas
4) Kero Refinerias de Maiz
5) 1983(Argentina)
6) deep red
943 1) perimeter weighting
system for tennis rackets
2),3) Osamu Furumura
4) Sony Wilson
5) 1982(Japan)
944 1) computer search
2),3) David Lock
4) Computer Search
5) 1988(England)
6) black/red/yellow
945 1) industry
3) Yoshimitsu Kato
4) Iccho Kogyo Co.,Ltd.
5) 1982(Japan)
946 1) real estate
development
2) João Carlos Cauduro/
Ludovico Antonio Martino
4) BFBA
5) 1981(Brazil)
947 1) computer
communications
2) Gottschalk & Ash
International
3) Peter Adam/Stuart Ash
4) Communications Seminar
5) 1977(Canada)
948 1) publisher
2),3) Jorge Sposari
4) Editorial ANESA
5) 1974(Argentina)
949 1) engines
2) Yuji Kano
3) Shigo Yamaguchi

4) Toyota
5) 1981(Japan)
950 1) wine restaurant
2) Takenobnu Igarashi
3) Yukimi Sasago/Takenobu
Igarashi
4) Restaurant Riposate
5) 1983(Japan)
951 1) dance studio
2) Peter Steiner
3) Michael Friedland
4) Focus Jazz
5) 1983(Canada)
6) blue
952 1) watches
2) Noboru Abe/Tetsuo Sato
3) Toshiyasu Nanbu
4) Matsushita Electric Works, Ltd.
5) 1981(Japan)
953 1) title of magazine
2) Konzo Nakagawa
3) Satoshi Morikami
4) Shin Kyoto Shinpan
5) 1983(Japan)
954 1) travel agency
3) Florent Garnier
4) Office de Tourisme de Lyon
5) 1983(France)
6) black/blue/white/red
955 1) confectionery
3) Helmut Schmidt
4) Ruban D'or
5) 1981(Japan)
6) DIC 554 →C24 · 25, M26-29
956 1) construction
consulting engineers
2),3) Stein Davidsen
4) Elliot Stromme
5) 1975(Norway)
6) blue
957 1) institute
3) Jan Hollender
4) Institute of Home Market
and Consumption
5) 1984(Poland)
958
2),3) Hans Kündig
4) Spar Vatten & Energi AB
5) 1983(Sweden)
6) black/red/blue
959 1) department store
2) Shunji Niinomi
3) Tetsuharu Mabuchi
4) Sunseven
5) 1976(Japan)
960 1) campaign(furniture)
2) Shigeo Ohashi
3) Takao Sasaki
4) Osawa & Co.,Ltd.
5) 1982(Japan)
961 1) pets(accessories)
2) Richard Wittosch
3) Richard Wittosch/Nicholas
Sinadinos
4) Noah's Ark Pet Centers
5) 1976(USA)
6) brown
962 1) anniversary
2),3) Dieter Urban
4) 2000 Jahre Stadt Augsburg
5) 1983(Belgium)
963 1) micro-cassette
recorder
2) Masami Akimoto/Zenjiro
Kurihara

3) Ikuo Masubuchi
4) Olympus
5) 1982(Japan)
964 1) publication
2),3) Shigo Yamaguchi
4) Swing Journal
5) 1983(Japan)
965 1) transportation
2),3) Walter Hergenröther
4) Trans Inter Continental Service
5) 1975(Italy)
6) light green/dark green
966 1) oil hot-water heater
2),3) Yoshihiko Kurobe
4) Ina Seito Co.,Ltd.
5) 1982(Japan)
967 1) T.V. sign(science
technical progress)
3) Nikola Nikolov
4) Bulgarian T.V.
5) 1976(Bulgaria)
6) black/white
968 1) interior(decorative
papers)
2),3) Guillermo Gonzalez Ruiz
4) Vinilia
5) 1979(Argentina)
969
2),3) Bill Wood
4) Hallmark, Inc.
5) 1980(USA)
6) redish purple/black
970 1) title of book
2),3) Hiroshi Toida
4) Geibunsha
5) 1980(Japan)
971 1) sport(children's
alpine skiing program)
2),3) Scott Engen
4) Solitude Ski Team
5) 1983(USA)
6) black/red(PMS 032)
972 1) confection
2),3) Gustavo Gomez
-Casallas/Rodrigo Fernandez
4) Ropita
5) 1979(colambia)
6) red/orange
973 1) unit furniture sale
2),3) Yoriya Ueda
4) Seibu Department Store
5) 1980(Japan)
974 1) auto parts
(manufacturer)
2) Yuji Sato
3) Takaaki Yoshinobu
4) Rimo
5) 1982(Japan)
975 1) canned fruit products
2) Fernando Rion
3) Fernando Rion/Aljandro
Raygados
4) Super Marcas
5) 1974(Mexico)
6) white/orange/yellow/
warm red
976
2),3) Carlos Roland
4) E. Romero Giron
5) 1979(Spain)
6) white/black
977 1) title of a magazine
article
3) Shigo Yamaguchi
4) Swing Journal Co.,Ltd.

5) 1981(Japan)
978 1) theater
2),3) Carlos Roland
4) Teatro Estable Castelland
5) 1974(Spain)
6) black/white
979 1) beach club(Acapulco)
2) Joe Vera
3) Francisco Tellez/Joe Vera
4) Ramada Inn
5) 1977(Mexico)
6) orange
980 1) farm
2),3) Terry Lesniewicz/Al Navarre
4) Fantasy Hill Farms Limited
5) 1983(USA)
981 1) clothing(women's
underwear)
2) Jiro Sawada
4) Wacoal
5) 1979(Japan)
982 1) blood donor center
2),3) Scott Engen
4) Metropolitan Blood Center
5) 1979(USA)
6) black/red(PMS 032)
983 1) records
2),3) Terry Lesniewicz/Al
Navarre
4) Boogie Records
5) 1977(USA)
984 1) sport
3) Ivan Dvoršak
4) Combine "Sport" Beograd
5) 1983(Yugoslavia)
6) blue
985
2),3) Ricardo Rey
4) Conzanez Padin Inc.
5) 1974(Puerto Rico)
6) full color
986
2),3) Ricardo Rey
4) Turi-Club, Inc.
5) 1976(Puerto Rico)
6) full color
987 1) cycling
2),3) Greg Siple
4) Scioto River Valley Bicycle
Tour
5) 1977(USA)
6) black
988 1) sport shop
2),3) Gustavo Gomez
-Casallas/Rodrigo Fernandez
4) Casa Olimpica
5) 1979(Colombia)
6) orange
989 1) TV film company
2),3) Carlos Rolando
4) Group Films International
5) 1976(Spain)
6) black/white
990 1) title of a section in a
publication
2) Carlos Rolando
3) Jose Carlos Rodriguez
4) Sal Comun(Rock Magazine)
5) 1978(Spain)
6) black/white
991 1) magazine
3) Paul Ibou
4) Vorm in Vlaanderen
5) 1982(Belgium)
992 1) cable television

4) Avanova International Ltd.
5) 1983(Sweden)
6) black
1049 1) congress(political party)
3) Stephan Kantscheff
4) 12th Congress of the Bulgarian Communist Party
5) 1980(Bulgaria)
1050 1) works company
3) A.G. Schillemans
4) M24 Dag & Nacht Service
5) 1978(Netherlands)
6) blue/purple/warm red
1051 1) auto parts(repair and sale)
3) Ken Design
4) Tanimura Jidosha
5) 1983(Japan)
1052 1) instrumental works
3) Stephan Kantscheff
4) Zinor
5) 1981(Bulgaria)
1053 1) beauty salon
2) Great Expectations Inc./N.Y.
3) Eishi Yamaguchi
4) Cut & Curl Japan
5) 1979(Japan)
1054 1) food store
2),3) Yoriya Ueda
4) Seibu Department Stores
5) 1976(Japan)
1055 1) kitchen utensils
2),3) Teruo Fujishige
4) Komeda Firm
5) 1981(Japan)
1056 1) cafe
2),3) Shunji Niinomi
4) Eau-De-Vie
5) 1982(Japan)
1057 1) Asian food service
2),3) Oanh Pham-Phu
4) Le Viet Sung
5) 1983(West Germany)
6) black/green
1058 1) restaurant
2),3) Erich Unger
4) 1973(West Germany)
5) black
1059 1) family restaurant
2),3) Hidemichi Yamao
4) Tokyo Flight Kitchen Co.,Ltd.
5) 1983(Japan)
6) DIC 565
1060 1) sporting goods
2),3) John M. Alexander
4) Mission Custom Golf Clubs
5) 1975(USA)
6) black
1061 1) cultural exhibition
2) T. A. Lewandowski
3) Jean Larcher
4) Banque d'Images
5) 1982(France)
6) black/white
1062 1) jeweler(campaign)
2) Kuniharu Masubuchi
3) Emiko Tachiyama/Hiroshi Iseya
4) Mikimoto Co.,Ltd.
5) 1982(Japan)
1063 1) woman's dress maker
2),3) Shunji Niinomi
4) Act-1
5) 1977(Japan)

1064 1) oil company
2),3) Walter Hergenröther
4) Petron Oil SpA
5) 1977(Italy)
6) blue/orange
1065
2),3) Terry Lesniewicz/Al Navarre
4) RPOD
5) 1983(USA)
1066 1) electric works company
2),3) Masahiro Abe
4) Daiwa Electric Work Co.,Ltd.
5) 1981(Japan)
6) DIC 162
1067 1) Irish linen maker
3) Richard Eckersley
4) John England Ltd.
5) 1979(Ireland)
6) white/brown
1068 1) motion picture (television)
2),3) Philip Gips/Diana Graham
4) National Captioning, Ltd.
5) 1979(USA)
6) black
1069 1) campaign
3) Kazunari Nishida
4) Shizuoka Railroad Co.,Ltd.
5) 1978(Japan)
1070 1) newsletter masthead
2),3) Bruce D. Zahor
4) The Art Director's Club of New York
5) 1980(USA)
6) black/white
1071 1) electric works company
2) Norihiko Watanabe
3) Mariko Ozawa
4) Ono Denki Sangyo Co.,Ltd.
5) 1981(Japan)
1072 1) monocycle
2),3) Sogen Onishi
4) Kuwabara Cars Co.,Ltd.
5) 1981(Japan)
6) black/yellow
1073 1) sports club(tennis)
2),3) Harry Murphy
4) Money Tennis
5) 1975(USA)
6) green
1074 1) tennis group
2),3) Yasaburo Kuwayama
4) Tennis Group Canardeaux
5) 1976(Japan)
6) white/gold
1075 1) tennis school
2),3) Shigeo Katsuoka
4) Sekimoto · Kawada Tennis School
5) 1981(Japan)
6) light green(DIC 173)
1076 1) title of a magazine article
2) Isao Kusumi
3) Kenzo Nakagawa
4) Good Days
5) (Japan)
1077 1) travel campaign
2) Iwao Miyanaga
3) Yasaburo Kuwayama
4) Seibu Travel

5) 1974(Japan)
1078 1) marine museum
2),3) Ricardo Rey
4) Museo del Mar Inc.
5) 1975(Puerto Rico)
6) ultramarine blue
1079 1) soft drinks
2) Takashi Fujita
3) Yoshio Kato
4) Suntory Ltd.
5) 1982(Japan)
1080 1) railroad service for skiers
2),3) David Leigh
4) Ski Train
5) 1972(USA)
6) dark blue
1081 1) golf accessories
2),3) Yoshihiro Yoshida
4) Irebun Shuppan
5) 1973(Japan)
1082 1) bowling alley
2),3) Ernesto Lehfeld
4) Bol Sanangel Bowling Alley
5) 1971(Mexico)
6) warm red
1083 1) shoe repair
2) Joe Selame
3) Selame Design Group
4) Fix'm Shoe Centers
5) 1980(USA)
6) red/brown
1084 1) photo studio
2) Hideki Aoki
3) Isao Ecchuya
4) Ad Angle
5) 1982(Japan)
1085 1) shoes
2),3) John S.Brown
4) Industrial Safety Equipment Co.
5) 1970(Canada)
6) green/blue
1086
2),3) Fernando Medina
4) Zapatonian
5) 1978(Spain)
6) yellow/green/blue
1087 1) T-shirt store
2),3) Harry Murphy
4) Shirtique
5) 1977(USA)
6) black/white
1088 1) photo studio
2),3) Katsuichi Ito
4) Mitani Studio
5) 1980(Japan)
1089 1) accessories shop
3) Kazuo Kanai
4) Voie
5) 1976(Japan)
1090 1) article in a public relations magazine
2),3) Yasaburo Kuwayama
4) Asahi Culture Center
5) 1975(Japan)
1091 1) textiles
2),3) Jorge Canales
4) Tercet de Mexico, S.A.
5) 1982(Mexico)
6) dark blue/gold
1092 1) association(rocketeers)
2),3) John D. Stewart
4) Paisley Rocketeers' Society
5) 1980(England)
6) blue
1093 1) camper body builder

2),3) Giovanni Brunazzi
4) Almo
5) 1976(Italy)
1094
2),3) Jagdish Chavda
4) Gla Picks
5) 1978(USA)
1095 1) discoteque
2),3) Tadasu Fukano
4) Shimoda Prince Hotel
5) 1973(Japan)
1096
3) Florent Garnier
4) Fondation Mérieux
5) 1983(France)
6) blue/white/red
1097 1) sport(club)
2),3) Bruce D. Zahor
4) Grand Central Racketball Club
5) 1982(USA)
6) green/brown/white
1098 1) movie title
2) Katsumi Yutani
3) Shigo Yamaguchi
4) Toho-Towa
5) 1980(Japan)
1099 1) land developer
2),3) Silvio Gayton
4) Resnick-Dunaevsky Land Developers
5) 1982(USA)
6) brown
1100 1) title of public relations bulletin
2) Ken'ichi Sakurai
3) Hideko Sakado
4) Shell Oil Co.
5) 1980(Japan)
1101 1) article in a public relations bulletin
2) Kuniharu Masubuchi
3) Hiroshi Iseya
4) Mikimoto Co.,Ltd.
5) 1981(Japan)
1102 1) pub restaurant
2),3) Kunihiko Ishikawa
4) American House
5) 1982(Japan)
6) C100 + M70
1103 1) restaurant
2) Lew Lehrman
3) Robin Smith
4) Star Indian Restaurant
5) 1976(USA)
1104 1) trade
3) Guido Redaelli
4) Socinter
5) 1978(Italy)
6) blue
1105 1) trade
2) João Carlos Cauduro/Ludovico Antonio Martino
4) Cicatrade
5) 1982(Brazil)
1106 1) publisher
2) Vera Salamounová
3) Jiri Rathousky
4) Panorama
5) 1977(Czechoslovakia)
1107 1) film studio
3) Stephan Kantscheff
4) Inter Film
5) 1974(Bulgaria)
1108 1) film production

2),3) Masaaki Fukuda
4) Taiho Co.,Ltd.
5) 1979(Japan)
1167 1) swimming school
3) Sergio Salaroli
4) Nuoto Imperi
5) 1979(Italy)
6) black/blue/yellow
1168 1) association(education)
2),3) Tony Forster
4) Bolton Dyslexia Association
5) 1981(England)
6) black/gray
1169 1) bank
2),3) F.R. Esteban
4) Pittsburgh National Bank
5) 1977(USA)
6) black
1170 1) church
2) F. R. Esteban
3) F. R. Esteban/Jeff Piatt
4) St. Stephen's Church
5) 1982(USA)
6) black
1171 1) ad campaign(holy week)
2),3) Joe Vera
4) Channel 13 Mexico
5) 1970(Mexico)
1172 1) furniture
3) Shigo Yamaguchi
4) Baba Furniture
5) 1976(Japan)
1173 1) textiles
3) Yasumasa Oka
4) Okahashi
5) 1976(Japan)
1174 1) wood-print
2),3) Yukihisa Takakita
4) Tokai TV Jigyo Co.,Ltd.
5) 1983(Japan)
1175 1) whisky
2) Shiro Kawahara
3) Yasaburo Kuwayama
4) Nikka Whisky
5) 1975(Japan)
6) black
1176 1) interior design
3) Masaharu Sumida
4) Yellow House
5) 1978(Japan)
1177 1) manufacturer of electric appliances
2),3) Minoru Takahashi
4) Sony
5) 1983(Japan)
1178 1) Building
3) Michael Herold
4) Theissen Inc.
5) 1980(West Germany)
6) black
1179 1) sandwich and tea garden
2) Shigeo Katsuoka
3) Shigeo Katsuoka/Hiroshi Asami
4) Miwa Gallery Co.,Ltd.
5) 1981(Japan)
6) dark blue(DIC 222)
1180 1) gallery
2),3) Diana Graham
4) Backdoor Art Gallery
5) 1975(USA)
6) black
1181 1) restaurant

2) Yoichi Sugamura
3) Michiko Sugamura
4) Hermes
5) 1981(Japan)
1182 1) advertising agency
2) John Harris
3) Tony Forster
4) Baglow Harris West & Partners
5) 1982(England)
6) brown
1183 1) textiles
2) Keith Murgatroyd
3) Tony Forster
4) Kiskadee Fabrics Ltd.
5) 1976(England)
6) dark green
1184 1) advertising agency
2) Harry Mills/Alan Wallis
3) Tony Forster
4) Mills Wallis & Allan Ltd.
5) 1978(England)
6) pale ochre
1185 1) publishing(photo book)
2) Akisato Ueda/Tsuneo Taniguchi/Nobuo Ohara
3) Akisato Ueda
4) Shinshindo
5) 1977(Japan)
1186 1) real estate
2) Iwao Miyanaga
3) Yasaburo Kuwayama
4) Seibu Fudosan
5) 1977(Japan)
1187 1) game package
2),3) Scott Engen
4) Stick It
5) 1978(USA)
6) black/silver
1188 1) accountants' office
2),3) Alvin Joe
4) John C. Lee Associates
5) 1980(USA)
6) terra cotta red/dark brown
1189 1) café lounge
2),3) Takao Yoguchi
4) Rap's
5) 1980(Japan)
1190 1) sports food
3) Shin Matsunaga
4) Meiji Seika Co.,Ltd.
5) 1979(Japan)
1191
2),3) Yoshihiro Yoshida
4) Shogyoshisetsu Kenkyusho
5) 1983(Japan)
1192 1) medical library
2),3) Joe Dieter
4) Welch Medical Library, Johns Hopkins Hospital
5) 1975(USA)
6) black
1193 1) bank card
2),3) James Lienhart
4) OMNI
5) (USA)
1194 1) magazine
2),3) James Lienhard
4) Success
5) (USA)
1195 1) radio station
2),3) James Lienhard
4) WBEZ
5) (USA)

1196 1) lighting manufacturer
2),3) Minoru Takahashi
4) Ushio Spax
5) 1980(Japan)
1197
2),3) Steve Shelden
4) J. D. Price
5) 1977(USA)
6) brown
1198 1) men's suits
2) Iwao Miyanaga
3) Yasaburo Kuwayama
4) Onward
5) 1975(Japan)
6) black
1199 1) private symbol(singers)
2) Shigo Yamaguchi
3) Shigo Yamaguchi/Masaki Furuta
4) Wings
5) 1983(Japan)
1200 1) alcoholic beverage (campaign)
2) Keisuke Nagatomo/Kenzo Nakagawa
3) Kenzo Nakagawa/Satoshi Morikami/Sumiko Tsuya
4) Suntory
5) 1980(Japan)
1201 1) alcoholic beverage (campaign)
2) Keisuke Nagatomo/Kenzo Nakagawa
3) Kenzo Nakagawa/Satoshi Morikami/Sumiko Tsuya
4) Suntory
5) 1980(Japan)
1202 1) restaurant
2),3) Minoru Takahashi
4) Osada Pacific
5) 1982(Japan)
1203 1) hotel
2) Toshio Goto
3) Hiroshi Shibuya
4) Ichirino Kogen Hotel
5) 1977(Japan)
6) green
1204 1) music(jazz band)
2),3) Tony Forster
4) Alexanders Ragtime Band
5) 1977(England)
6) black
1205 1) propaganda
2),3) Yoshiari Hirano
4) International Micro Technology
5) 1983(Japan)
1206 1) travel agency
3) Yoneo Jinbo
4) World Plan
5) 1981(Japan)
1207 1) market
2),3) Milton Glaser
4) Heartland Market;Crown Center Redevelopment Corp.
5) 1982-83(USA)
6) blue/pink
1208 1) snack
2),3) Yoshihiro Yoshida
4) Shendy
5) 1979(Japan)
1209 1) religious organization
2),3) Joe Dieter
4) Maryland Bible Society

5) 1979(USA)
6) white/gold
1210
2),3) Denise Spaulding
4) Mid-America Federal
5) 1982(USA)
6) red/blue
1211 1) campaign
2) Walter Wardell/Jurek Wajdowicz
3) Jurex Wajdowicz
4) New York Telephone
5) 1983(USA)
6) blue/red/white
1212 1) food
2),3) Takao Yoguchi
4) Toppan-Printing
5) 1977(Japan)
6) black
1213
2),3) Hans Kündig
4) Friskvards Centrum
5) 1983(Sweden)
6) black/blue/green/yellow
1214 1) publication (catalogue)
2) Carlos Rolando
3) Ricardo Rousselot
4) I. P. Magazine
5) 1977(Spain)
6) black/green/orange
1215 1) golf accessories
2),3) Yoshihiro Yoshida
4) Seikeido
5) 1982(Japan)
1216
2),3) Michael Baviera
4) ALOS
5) 1980(Switzerland)
6) red/black
1217 1) coffee shop
2),3) Hiroshi Komai
4) Doji House
5) 1980(Japan)
1218 1) jeweler
2),3) Norberto Coppola
4) Guthmann
5) 1970(Argentina)
6) gold/silver
1219 1) electronic machine
2) Marty Neumeier
3) Sandra Higashi
4) Braegen Corporation
5) 1983(USA)
6) gray
1220 1) credit card
2) João Carlos Cauduro/Ludovico Antonio Martino
4) Credicard S.A.
5) 1982(Brazil)
1221 1) organization serving the deaf
2),3) David Leigh
4) American Professional Society of the Deaf
5) 1973(USA)
6) turquoise
1222 1) vehicle identification
2),3) Jack Weiss
4) City of Evanston, Illinois
5) 1978(USA)
6) blue/green
1223 1) printing
2),3) Yasaburo Kuwayama
4) Shiko Insatsu

4) Kissan Products
5) 1975(India)
6) blue
1283
3) Werner Schneider
4) Kunst-Guss Eschenburg
5) 1978(West Germany)
6) brown
1284 1) restaurant
2),3) James Lienhart
4) Federal Street Cafe
5) 1984(USA)
1285 1) boutique
2) Nobuyoshi Shigematsu
3) Tadashi Yoshimatsu
4) Rocovis
5) 1982(Japan)
1286
2),3) Milton Glaser
4) Grand Union Company
5) 1983(USA)
6) dark green/pink/ocher
1287 1) entertainment
(exhibition)
2),3) Yukihisa Takakita
4) 1983(Japan)
1288 1) poster, magazine
advertisement
2),3) Ben Nakanishi
4) Mochizuki Kasugadaira
Country Club
5) 1976(Japan)
1289 1) bookstore
3) Hermann Zapf
4) Hermann Emig Bookstore
5) 1977(West Germany)
6) red or blue
1290 1) food(manufacturer)
2),3) Eduardo A. Cánovas
4) Euralim S.A.
5) 1983(Argentina)
6) green/red/black
1291 1) agricultural
equipment(manufacturer)
2) Philip J. Turner
3) Eurographic Ltd.
4) Weeks Trailers Ltd.
5) 1974(England)
6) blue
1292 1) printing company
2),3) David Gibbs
4) Walnut Circle Press
5) 1979(USA)
6) embossed
1293 1) real estate broker
2) Jurek Wajdowicz
3) Jurek Wajdowicz/Ted
Szumilas
4) Kanelba & Robilotti
5) 1983(USA)
6) PMS 303
1294 1) publication
3) Hermann Zapf
4) Carl Hanser Verlag
5) 1970(West Germany)
1295 1) automobile
accessories
2) Yoichi Sugamura
3) Michiko Sugamura
4) Monte Carlo
5) 1976(Japan)
1296 1) printing company
2) Jack Evans
3) Unigraphics, Inc.
4) Spruiell & Company

5) 1982(USA)
6) tan
1297
2),3) Milton Glaser
4) Towers of Quaside(The
Great House)/Joseph Baum
Company
5) 1981(USA)
6) red/yellow/green blue/
black
1298 1) food
2) Robert P. Gersin
3) Pamela Virgilio
4) Government of Jamaica
5) 1983(USA)
6) white → C127
1299 1) food company
2) Julia Ganda
3) Rabecca Bouling
4) Doris Louise Catering
5) 1984(USA)
6) red/ochre
1300 1) photo studio
2),3) David Leigh
4) Neikrug Galleries, Inc.
5) 1979(USA)
6) gray
1301 1) cultural poster
2) Franck Vardon
3) Jean Larcher
4) ERATO
5) 1981(France)
6) black/white
1302 1) picture gallery
2),3) Jack Weiss
4) Neville-Sargent Gallery
5) 1981(USA)
6) warm gray(PMS 408)
1303 1) design studio
2) Jack Weiss
3) Randi Robin
4) Disign Information, Inc.
5) 1982(USA)
6) blue(PMS 285)
1304 1) liquor
2) John DiGianni
3) Gianninoto Associates, Inc.
4) The Jos. Garneau Company
5) 1983(USA)
6) gold/deep green
1305 1) advertising agency
2),3) Scott Engen
4) Haute Ayer Adv. P. R.
5) 1983(USA)
6) black
1306 1) department store
(men's wear)
3) Yutaka Mitani
4) Seibu Department Stores
5) 1980(Japan)
1307 1) restaurant
2),3) Kaoru Iida
4) Swing
5) 1978(Japan)
1308
2),3) Armin Vogt
4) Infomal
5) 1977(Switzerland)
6) black
1309 1) furnace
(manufacturer)
2),3) Joe Dieter
4) The Heat Machine
5) 1971(USA)
6) orange

1310
2),3) Pietro Galli
4) Saturnia
5) 1968(Italy)
6) gold/blue
1311 1) restaurant
2),3) Bruce D. Zahor
4) Bechet's Restaurant Inc.
5) 1980(USA)
6) dark red/white
1312
2),3) PVDI
4) Empresas Atalla
5) 1973(Brazil)
1313 1) textile industry
2) Ricardo Salas
3) Alejandra Rodriguez
4) D'Velvet
5) (Mexico)
6) red/violet
1314 1) department store
(press sheet for information)
2),3) Yoriya Ueda
4) Seibu Department Stores
Information
5) 1979(Japan)
6) Seibu corporate blue(DIC
183)
1315 1) movie studio
2),3) Milton Glaser
4) Zoetrope Studios/Francis
Ford Coppola
5) 1981(USA)
6) embossed
1316 1) hotel
2),3) Silvio Gayton
4) Eden Roc Hotel
5) 1982(USA)
6) burgundy lake/black
1317 1) restaurant
2) Alfonso Capetillo Ponce
3) Ricardo Salas
4) Restaurante Metal Bar
5) 1981(Mexico)
6) black/yellow/blue
1318 1) publication
2),3) Jurek Wajdowicz
4) Dollar Stock Journal
5) 1983(USA)
6) black
1319 1) concert promotion
2),3) Scott Engen
4) KUER FM 90 Radio USA
5) 1983(USA)
6) black
1320 1) stationery
2),3) John Stevens
4) Paper for Pens
5) 1981(USA)
1321 1) publication
(educational magazine)
2),3) Scott Engen
4) University of
Utah(Instructional Media
Services)
5) 1982(USA)
6) black
1322 1) building(symbol)
3) Shin Matsunaga
4) Shinjuku Station Building
5) 1978(Japan)
6) red(DIC 565)
1323 1) restaurant
2),3) Milton Glaser
4) Rudi's Country Kitchen

5) 1976(USA)
6) dark brown/crome yellow/
red
1324 1) food(manufacturer)
2) George Delany
3) Sandra Delany
4) Kilvert & Forbes
5) 1980(USA)
6) deep red
1325 1) glasses
2) Shigeo Oohashi
3) Hidehiko Inui/Osamu Oto/
Rei Fujita
4) Ishiyama Glasses
5) 1982(Japan)
1326 1) boutique
2),3) Terry Lesniewicz/Al
Navarre
4) The Emporium
5) 1981(USA)
1327 1) gun club
2),3) Don Davis
4) Great River Gun Club
5) 1971(USA)
6) black/gray
1328
2),3) Thomas J. Ambrosino
4) Brother Jacks
5) 1983(USA)
6) black/white
1329 1) sport(baton studio)
2) Mieko Mizumori
3) Muneo Mizumori
4) Twin Baton Studio
5) 1982(Japan)
1330
2),3) Steve Allen
4) Dixie States Enterprises, Inc.
5) 1981(USA)
6) brown
1331
2),3) Thomas J. Ambrosino
4) The Place
5) 1983(USA)
6) black/white
1332 1) recording studio
2),3) Carlos Rolando
4) Rafael Turia
5) 1976(Spain)
6) dark brown
1333 1) bookstore
2),3) Christof Gassner
4) Vera Kopp
5) 1980(West Germany)
1334 1) market
2),3) Milton Glaser
4) Heartland Market/Crown
Center Redevelopment Corp.
5) 1982(USA)
6) ocher/yellow/terra-cotta/
dark green
1335 1) liquor
2),3) Carlo Malerba
4) Robba Rocco Spa
5) 1976(Italy)
1336 1) antique shop
2) Jack Weiss
3) Randi Robin
4) Miller & Schweizer
5) 1983(USA)
6) gold/dark green(PMS 343)
1337 1) entertainment
(exhibition)
2) Shigeo Katsuoka
3) Shigeo Katsuoka/Hiroshi

5) 1981(Japan)
1395 1) mobile phone service
2) Ichiro Saito
3) Ichiro Saito/Jiro Minowa
4) Japan Mobile Phone Service
5) 1979(Japan)
1396 1) shoe repair
2),3) Mo Lebowitz
4) Cobbler's Bench
5) 1983(USA)
6) black
1397 1) construction, real estate
2),3) Oanh Pham-Phu
4) Prinz von Anhalt
5) 1982(West Germany)
6) blue
1398 1) discoteque
2) Fernando Rión
3) Frank Carr
4) Operatec, S.A.
5) 1982(Mexico)
6) orange(Pantone 65C)/black
1399 1) discoteque
2) Fernando Rión
3) Frank Carr
4) Operatec, S.A.
5) 1982(Mexico)
6) orange(Pantone 65C)/black
1400
2),3) David Gibbs
4) Graphic House
5) 1978(USA)
6) black
1401 1) university
3) Gerd Fleischmann
4) University Bielefeld
5) 1982(West Germany)
6) blue/yellow/silver
1402 1) printed matter
2),3) Herbert Wenn
4) Emhart House publication
5) 1981(West Germany)
6) black/white
1403 1) railroad
2) Velizar Petrov
3) Bulgarian State Railways
4) 1972(Bulgaria)
1404 1) motor oil
2) Tadashi Ishikawa
3) Kazunari Nishida
4) Zen-No
5) 1980(Japan)
1405 1) information
2),3) Don Connelly
4) North American Newstime
5) 1981(USA)
1406 1) swimming pool
2),3) Tadasu Fukano
4) Hotel White Town
5) 1974(Japan)
1407 1) tea room
2),3) Shuji Torigoe
4) Parlour Maupiti
5) 1971(Japan)
1408 1) fruit and vegetable store
2),3) Shuji Torigoe
4) Mitsuba Store
5) 1974(Japan)
1409
2) Gottschalk & Ash International
3) Stuart Ash
4) Rolph-McNally Limited

5) 1977(Canada)
1410 1) underground market
2),3) Akisato Ueda
4) Osaka Underground Center
5) 1976(Japan)
1411 1) design studio
2) Greg Resler
3) Mike Leidel
4) John H. Harland Co.
5) 1982(USA)
6) green
1412 1) store(fur)
3) Shigetoshi Shibata
4) Yoshinoto
5) 1982(Japan)
1413 1) restaurant
2),3) Minoru Takahashi
4) 1979(Japan)
1414 1) association of consultant engineers
2),3) PVDI
4) Explan
5) (Brazil)
1415 1) restaurant(pizza)
2),3) Carlos Rolando
4) El Forn de la Pizza
5) 1981(Spain)
6) green/red/yellow
1416 1) association(bingo)
2),3) Bruce D. Zahor
4) Bingo Buyers Association
5) 1984(USA)
6) black/white
1417
3) Daphne Duijvelshoff
4) Aspémar, Brussels
5) 1982(Netherlands)
6) black
1418 1) movie(title)
2) József Marx
3) György Kemény
4) Hun Garofilm
5) 1981(Hungary)
6) black/white
1419 1) design(production)
2),3) Yoriya Ueda
4) Nobu
5) 1974(Japan)
1420 1) trailer rental
3) Kenneth Hollick
4) Commercial Sale & Lease Ltd.
5) 1982(England)
6) red/blue
1421 1) photo studio
2) Robert P. Gersin
3) Scott Bolestridge
4) Hi-Tech
5) 1983(USA)
6) black/white/magenta
1422
2) Renato Gomes
3) Alicia Marina Osborne
4) Ziggy Ltda
5) 1978(Brazil)
6) red
1423 1) frozen food
2) Philip J. Turner
3) Eurographic Ltd.
4) TFC Foods Ltd.
5) 1977(England)
6) any single color or multicolor
1424
2) P. Cayton
3) Mike Quon

4) American Baby Cable
5) 1983(USA)
6) black/white
1425 1) computer company
2) Jack Weiss
3) Carter Clock
4) Compro
5) 1978(USA)
6) rust
1426 1) sporting goods
2) Jack Weiss
3) Randi Robin
4) Steven-Marsh Company
5) 1978(USA)
6) blue
1427 1) boutique
2) Shigeru Shimooka
3) Toyohiko Sugimoto
4) Miki
5) 1983(Japan)
6) black/white
1428 1) department store(household utensils)
2),3) Yoriya Ueda
4) Seibu Department Stores
5) 1975(Japan)
1429 1) magazine title
2),3) Shin Matsunaga
4) Fashion Current
5) 1977(Japan)
1430 1) fashion boutique
2) Tadao Oonuki
3) Muneo Mizumori
4) Matsuzakaya
5) 1970(Japan)
1431 1) private symbol (photographer)
2),3) R & S Baur
4) M. Folliet
5) 1983(Switzerland)
6) black → M36
1432 1) computer
2),3) Richard Yeager
4) Kalbro Computer Corporation
5) 1979(USA)
6) black/white
1433 1) management magazine association
2),3) Norberto Coppola
4) Instituto para la Integración de América Latina
5) 1978(Argentina)
6) black/red
1434 1) anti-nuclear movement
2),3) Anthony O'Hanlon
4) Irishi Anti-Nuclear Movement
5) 1981(Ireland)
6) black/red
1435 1) publication(series)
3) Rosmarie Tissi
4) Arche Verlag
5) 1983(Switzerland)
6) black/red
1436 1) garage
2),3) Lanny Sommese
4) Lemont Garage
5) 1977(USA)
6) black/red → M37
1437 1) cream
2),3) Yasaburo Kuwayama
4) Meiji Dairy Industry
5) 1974(Japan)

6) black/white
1438 1) magazine title
2),3) Yasuhiko Shibukawa
4) Sanwa Publishing
5) 1981(Japan)
1439 1) toy(manufacturer)
3) István Szekeres
4) Játékstudió
5) 1979(Hungary)
6) black/gold
1440 1) record title
2) Gai Muranaka
3) Koji Takahashi
4) Victor Invitation
5) 1983(Japan)
1441 1) off road racing feature movie
2) Calvin Woo
3) Calvin Woo/Mike Hagstrom
4) Dirt
5) 1979(USA)
6) full color/black/white
1442 1) restaurant(fast food)
2),3) Carlos Rolando
4) Piscolabis
5) 1975(Spain)
6) black/white
1443 1) ballet school
2) Micheal Richards
3) Bill Swensen
4) The Ballet School at the University of Utah
5) 1980(USA)
1444 1) mail order(brand)
2),3) Hiro Terao
4) Hi-Sense
5) 1980(Japan)
1445 1) textile (product packages)
2),3) Masahiro Abe
4) Ichiei
5) 1982(Japan)
1446 1) hall
2),3) Calvert Guthrie
4) Parody Hall
5) 1982(USA)
6) blue/silver
1447 1) hall
2),3) Calvert Guthrie
4) Parody Hall
5) 1982(USA)
6) marine blue/midnight blue/silver/gray
1448
2),3) Don Davis
4) Carl Matson
5) 1974(USA)
6) black/gray
1449 1) coffee house
2),3) Osamu Ogawa
4) Kanazawa New Grand Hotel
5) 1973(Japan)
1450 1) toy
3) Stephan Kantshceff
4) Mucana Toy Shop
5) 1972(Bulgaria)
1451
2),3) Don Davis
4) Ven-Dall Corp.
5) 1974(USA)
6) green
1452 1) food
2),3) Koichi Watanabe
4) Nippon Meat Packers
5) 1977(Japan)

2),3) Kazuo Oono
4) Tokyu Agency
5) 1979(Japan)
1514 1) shoe(manufacturer)
2) Nobuyoshi Nakanishi
3) Yoshio Hirano
4) Achilles
5) 1979(Japan)
1515 1) cosmetic
2) The Planning Department of the Head Shop of Yanagiya
3) Yoshihiro Kishimoto
4) The Head Shop of Yanagiya
5) 1982(Japan) → C141
1516 1) cigarette
2),3) Oanh Pham-Phu
4) Philip Morris
5) 1980(West Germany)
1517 1) cocktail(label)
3) Eiko Sakata
4) Suntory
5) 1983(Japan)
1518
2) Jurek Wajdowicz
3) Ted Szumilas/Jurek Wajdodwicz
4) Innocenta Fashion Designer
5) 1981(USA)
6) silver
1519 1) entertainment (exhibition)
2),3) Shunji Kanda
4) Aron Chemical Synthesis
5) 1980(Japan)
6) blue(M10 + C100)
1520 1) printed matter
2) Yoshiharu Ito
3) Muneo Mizumori
4) Nagasakiya
5) 1979(Japan)
1521 1) apartment house
2),3) Kazuo Oono
4) Marubeni
5) 1978(Japan)
1522 1) jeweler
2) Ove Engström
3) Torgny Gustavsson
4) Jeweller's
5) 1981(Sweden)
6) black/silver
1523 1) women's designerwear
2),3) Toshiyasu Nanbu
4) Mode Pink
5) 1977(Japan)
1524 1) private symbol(fashion model)
2) Martin Nunn
3) Tony Foster
4) Barbara Lakeman
5) 1977(England)
6) brown
1525 1) private
3) Iwao Yamaguchi
4) Yoshiharu Suzuki
5) 1981(Japan)
1526
2),3) Arthur Echstein
4) Gold Seal Riviera Corporation
5) 1979(USA)
6) red(PMS 185)
1527
2),3) Henri-Paul Bronsard
4) Casavant et Frères Limitée

5) 1978(Canada)
6) burgundy
1528 1) hotel
2),3) Claude Dietrich
4) Hotel Crillon
5) 1980(Peru)
1529 1) association(children adoption)
2),3) Henri-Paul Bronsard
4) Organism Bénévole d' Adoption d'Enfants
5) 1982(Canada)
6) orange
1530 1) cosmetics (manufacturer)
2) Yoshihiro Yoshida
3) BEU Co.,Ltd.
4) 1980(Japan)
1531 1) poster
2) Lotus Engel
3) Jean Larcher
4) Palm
5) 1983(France)
6) white/gray
1532 1) hotel(cafeteria)
2),3) Claud Dietrich
4) Hotel Crillon
5) 1980(Peru)
1533
2),3) Joseph M. Bass
4) Decorative Laminates Ltd.
5) 1970-83(Israel)
1534 1) restaurant
2),3) Claude Dietrich
4) La Crêperie
5) (Peru)
1535 1) restaurant
2) Gottschalk & Ash International
3) Peter Adam
4) Griffin's Restaurant
5) 1980(Canada)
1536 1) furniture store
2),3) Tsuyoshi Miyake
4) Katayama Kaguten
5) 1977(Japan)
1537 1) clothing(brand)
2) Syozo Murase
3) Jun Yoshida/Toshinori Nozaki
4) Tulip Minoya
5) 1979(Japan)
1538 1) lounge
2),3) Tadasu Fukano
4) Shimoda Prince Hotel
5) 1973(Japan)
1539 1) boutique
2) Masahiro Shimizu
3) Jurie
5) 1982(Japan)
1540 1) music
2),3) Stein Davidsen
4) Hornaas Musikk
5) 1980(Norway)
6) black
1541 1) dry goods store
2),3) Syuji Torigoe
4) Hanezawaya
5) 1981(Japan)
1542 1) art gallery
2) Ziane
3) Jean Larcher
4) Orient Gallerie
5) 1983(France)
6) yellow/red

1543 1) church
2),3) Manfred Wutke
4) St. Bonifaz Church
5) 1980(West Germany)
6) brown
1544 1) textiles
2) Yukio Ishihara
3) Masahiro Shimizu
4) Thomas Itooka Co.,Ltd.
5) 1975(Japan)
1545 1) club
2) Renato Gomes
3) Eduardo Monteiro
4) Jazz Mania
5) 1983(Brazil)
6) gray
1546 1) private symbol (entertainer)
2) Joe Vera
3) Hector Sanchez
4) Peerless Records
5) 1980(Mexico)
1547
2) Renato Gomez
3) Nato Gomez
4) Fios e Formas
5) 1983(Brazil)
6) blue
1548 1) clothing(children's fashion shop)
3) Nair Iannibelli/Luiz Carlos Boeckel
4) Carolina Baby
5) 1983(Brazil)
1549 1) framing shop
2),3) Jean Larcher
4) Marie-Louise
5) 1982(France)
6) black/white
1550 1) restaurant
2) Alain Escot
3) Jean Larcher
4) La Boite Aux Lettres
5) 1983(France)
6) light brown
1551 1) antique shop
2),3) Jean Larcher
4) L'Etendard
5) 1983(France)
6) brown
1552 1) cultural association
2) Lotus Engel
3) Jean Larcher
4) Palm
5) 1983(France)
6) brown
1553 1) pen collector's club
2) Lionel Van Cleem
3) Jean Larcher
4) Club Des Collectionneurs De Plumes Et Object D'Écritures
5) 1982(France)
6) black/white
1554
2) Jerry L. Martin
3) Constance Chavez
4) Harris' Company
5) 1982(USA)
6) black
1555 1) mens clothing
2),3) Othmar Motter
4) Beck Herrenmoden
5) 1981(Austria)
6) black/white
1556 1) florist

3) Yoshikatsu Tami
4) Sonogi
5) 1982(Japan)
1557 1) confectionery
2),3) Yasumasa Oka
4) Bonforét
5) 1980(Japan)
1558 1) shopping center
2) Yoshihiro Saito
3) Shigo Yamaguchi
4) Sunshine City
5) 1981(Japan)
1559 1) theatre
2) Goran Cvetković
3) Jovica Veljović
4) Raskorak for performance "Rašomon"
5) 1983(Yugoslavia)
6) red
1560 1) theatre
2) Goran Cvetković
3) Jovica Veljović
4) Raskorak
5) 1982(Yugoslavia)
6) purple
1561 1) boutique
2) Shigeru Shimooka
3) Shigeru Shimooka/Masanobu Watanabe
4) Miki Corp.
5) 1983(Japan)
1562 1) publication
2),3) Gerd Leufert
4) Titular
5) 1977(Venezuela)
6) black
1563 1) design studio
2) Bob Ferguson
3) Guy Giunta
4) The Graphic Eye
5) 1982(USA)
6) white/black
1564 1) men's haberdashery
2),3) Fumio Koyoda
4) Sanwa Seni Co.,Ltd.
5) 1973(Japan)
1565
2),3) Cliff Chandler
4) John H. Harland Co.
5) 1983(USA)
1566 1) paper made tableware
2),3) Guy Giunta
4) Hallmark Cards, Inc.
5) 1982(USA)
6) black
1567 1) title of a magazine article
2),3) Shigo Yamaguchi
4) Swing Journal Co.,Ltd.
5) 1982(Japan)
1568 1) fashion show
2) Kansai Yamamoto
3) Shigo Yamaguchi
4) Kansai Super Studio
5) 1979(Japan)
1569 1) information bulletin
2) Moriyoshi Iijima
3) Kaoru Kasai
4) Japan Travel Bureau Co.,Ltd.
5) 1974(Japan)
1570 1) paper products
2) Keiichi Takahashi
3) Toshio Fukuyama
4) Daiichi Shiko
5) 1983(Japan)

fashion)
2) Shunji Niinomi
3) Tetsuharu Mabuchi
4) Polfin Co.,Ltd.
5) 1975(Japan)
1630 1) publication
2),3) Stephan Kantscheff
4) Bossyr
5) 1972(Bulgaria)
1631
2),3) Stephan Kantscheff
4) Rodopa
5) 1970(Bulgaria)
1632
2),3) Keijiro Ozumi
4) Joli Chapeau
5) 1982(Japan)
1633 1) manufacturer of baby products
2),3) Eduardo A. Canovas
4) Bebesit S.A.
5) 1980(Argentina)
6) violet
1634 1) institute(publication)
2),3) Giovanni Brunazzi
4) GESBE, Bergamo
5) 1976(Italy)
1635 1) private symbol (designer)
3) Miloš Ćirić
4) Miloš Ćirić
5) 1971(Yugoslavia)
1636 1) communication design & planning company
2) Jack Weiss
3) Randi Robin
4) Jack Weiss Associates, Inc.
5) 1980(USA)
6) blue/red/yellow/gray
1637 1) private symbol(stylist)
2),3) Minato Ishikawa
4) Masami Nakamura
5) 1975(Japan)
6) red/green
1638 1) leisure time equipment
2) Shnji Niinomi
3) Tetsuharu Mabuchi
4) Actum
5) 1982(Japan)
1639 1) building company
3) Peter Skalar
4) Vegrad
5) 1982(Yugoslavia)
6) black/brown
1640 1) art supplies
2),3) Tor Pettersen
4) Boardroom Paper and Board Storage System
5) 1974(England)
6) brown
1641 1) cosmetic products
2) Robert P. Gersin
3) R. Vanderberg
4) Shiseido Ltd.
5) 1982(USA)
6) silver
1642
2) Tom Lewis
3) Linda Roberts/Ann von Gal
4) Resource One
5) 1983(USA)
1643 1) bar restaurant
2) Yasaburo Kuwayama
3) Takaaki Yoshinobu

4) Gontran
5) 1978(Japan)
1644
3) Carlo Malerba
4) Luigi Bosca & F. spa
5) 1973(Italy)
1645 1) bar
2),3) Tadasu Fukano
4) Hotel New Otani
5) 1974(Japan)
1646 1) cosmetics
2),3) Katja Zelinka
4) Naj Naj Cosmetics
5) 1980(Yugoslavia)
6) violet
1647 1) bar
2),3) Tadasu Fukano
4) Naeba Prince Hotel
5) 1973(Japan)
1648 1) night club
2),3) Tadasu Fukano
4) Hotel Whitetown
5) 1974(Japan)
1649 1) ski club
2),3) Minato Ishikawa
4) Keio University Demonstration Ski Club
5) 1980(Japan)
1650 1) toys
2) Philip J. Turner
3) Eurographic Ltd.
4) Brenda Falconer
5) 1977(England)
1651 1) newspaper
2),3) Henri-Paul Bronsard
4) SODEP Inc.
5) 1974(Canada)
6) blue
1652 1) musical exhibition
3) Ricardo Blanco
4) Expomusica
5) 1977(Argentina)
6) green/red
1653 1) title of a magazine article
2) Isao Kusumi
3) Kenzo Nakagawa/Takashi Miyoshi
4) Magazine "Good Days"
5) (Japan)
1654 1) musical instrument(keyboard)
2),3) Shigeo Katsuoka
4) Nihon Gakki Seizo Co.,Ltd.
5) 1982(Japan)
1655 1) hotel
2),3) Tadasu Fukano
4) Hotel Whitetown
5) 1974(Japan)
1656
3) Jan Hollender
4) Elton
5) (Poland)
1657 1) construction(survey)
2) Ray Engle
3) Shannon Heiman
4) Southern California Edison Company
5) 1981(USA)
6) black
1658 1) food(seasoning)
2) Osamu Kato
3) Tsuyokatsu Kudo
4) Takeda Yakuhin Kogyo Co.,Ltd.
5) 1980(Japan)

1659 1) food(seasoning)
2) Osamu Kato
3) Tsuyokatsu Kudo
4) Takeda Yakuhin Kogyo Co.,Ltd.
5) 1980(Japan)
1660 1) cake(package)
2),3) Hidemichi Yamao
4) Sun Merry Co.,Ltd.
5) 1979(Japan)
1661 1) candy
2) Iwao Miyanaga
3) Yasaburo Kuwayama
4) Meiji Seika Co.,Ltd.
5) 1974(Japan)
6) black/white
1662 1) clothing(shop)
2),3) Stephan Kantscheff
4) Zubige Dorbutin
5) 1982(Bulgaria)
1663 1) printing company
2),3) Ernesto Lehfeld
4) Industrial Papelera Nacional
5) 1975(Mexico)
6) PMS 403
1664
2),3) Klaus Schmidt
4) Chardou
5) 1981(England)
1665 1) slogan
2),3) Jan Rajlich
4) Cesky Svaz Vyrobnich Druzstev Prague
5) 1978(Czechoslovakia)
1666
3) H. J. Burgert
4) 1971(West Germany)
6) black
1667
2) Michael Baviera
3) Rudi Baur
4) Seba Cliché & Offset
5) 1976(Switzerland)
6) yellow
1668 1) imported interior goods & gift shop
2),3) Akira Fukuda
4) Unisupply Ltd.
5) 1983(Japan)
1669 1) interior(storm door & window retailer)
2) Jack Weiss
3) Diana Lifton
4) The Bockman Company
5) 1979(USA)
6) silver
1670 1) shopping center
2),3) Takenobu Igarashi
4) Komatsubara Kenshu Jigyodan Co.,Ltd.
5) 1982(Japan)
1671 1) printing
2),3) Toshiyasu Nanbu
4) Unick Co.,Ltd.
5) 1972(Japan)
1672 1) interior design
3) Ricardo Blanco
4) Impacto S.A.
5) 1977(Argentina)
6) green
1673 1) record jacket
2) Sadayuki Masuda
3) Takenobu Igarashi
4) Canyon Records Inc.
5) 1982(Japan)
1674 1) record jacket

2) Sadayuki Masuda
3) Takenobu Igarashi
4) Canyon Records Inc.
5) 1982(Japan)
1675 1) coffee distributer
2),3) Raul Shakespear/Ronald Shakespear
4) Cafetal SAIC
5) 1976(Argentina)
6) brown
1676 1) printing
2),3) PVDI
4) Imprinta Fotocomposicçao e Off-set
5) 1971(Brazil)
1677
2),3) Matjaz Vipotnik
4) Andrea Jakil spa
5) 1979(Yugoslavia)
6) black
1678 1) audio visual group
2),3) Tony Forster
4) Multi Media Services International
5) 1983(England)
6) blue
1679 1) book store
3) Fernando Medina
4) Peter Bach
5) 1983(Spain)
6) orange/red
1680 1) title of a magazine article
2) Shigo Yamaguchi
3) Toshiko Nagano
4) Swing Journal Co.,Ltd.
5) 1983(Japan)
1681 1) title of a publication article
2),3) Shigo Yamaguchi
4) Swing Journal Co.,Ltd.
5) 1983(Japan)
1682 1) department store
2) Hidehiko Inui
3) Osamu Oto
4) Seibu Dept. Store
5) 1982(Japan)
1683 1) department store(accessories shop)
2) Yoriya Ueda
3) Hidekazu Honda
4) Seibu Dept. Store
5) 1980(Japan)
1684 1) food(delicatessen)
2),3) Georg Staehelin
4) Delicatessen Zur Münz
5) 1980(Switzerland)
6) dark green/pink
1685 1) gift shop
2),3) Chermayeff & Geismar Associates
4) Truc, Inc.
5) (USA)
6) black
1686 1) junk dealer
2),3) Lanny Sommese
4) Joe Junk
5) 1982(USA)
6) blue/white

Category Index

Category Index

music (sound apparatus)
56,100,130,182,197,259,262,312,337,351,362,432,470,
472,512,531,532,574,592,600,634,655,763,887,927,963,
983,1052,1204,1252,1253,1278,1319,1332,1342,1440,1540,
1577,1613,1618,1654,1673,1674,1678

recreational centers (zoos/botanical gardens)
1148,1339,1398,1399,1453,1457,1595,1616,1637

sports/sporting goods
41,45,48,61,113,123,158,171,365,422,486,547,567,571,
576,647,653,656,736,784,815,835,873,933,943,951,971,
984,987,988,1060,1073,1074,1075,1081,1082,1097,1161,
1167,1210,1215,1246,1328,1369,1426,1471,1474,1482

photography (photo studios)
89,253,277,314,356,35C,442,696,735,838,1084,1088,
1107,1143,1300,1421

printing/paper (packaging materials)
12,70,139,145,157,166,177,225,226,227,228,455,519,
534,543,582,613,623,624,635,645,657,662,732,777,
840,893,916,964,1070,1166,1187,1214,1223,1264,1292,
1296,1301,1402,1390,1454,1456,1487,1496,1501,1520,1531,
1566,1570,1579,1580,1581,1585,1587,1609,1626,1640,
1663,1671,1676

publications (bookstores)
16,35,84,149,250,275,289,305,320,352,364,375,405,
406,410,444,454,465,461,475,482,513,552,553,555,597,
598,599,607,614,625,739,751,772,773,785,789,809,826,
829,870,884,896,935,936,948,953,970,977,990,991,
993,1022,1076,1106,1147,1155,1185,1194,1228,1242,1243,
1251,1258,1260,1289,1294,1318,1321,1333,1361,1368,1386,
1429,1435,1438,1455,1468,1473,1480,1481,1500,1562,
1567,1569,1576,1593,1603,1610,1620,1624,1630,1634,
1653,1679,1680,1681

news (broadcasting newspaper)
87,211,252,315,324,503,546,572,636,649,967,992,1109,
1123,1174,1195,1405,1625,1651

communication (mail/telephone)
13,32,153,493,812,923,1137,1211,1395

transportation (air/sea)
9,75,180,397,578,695,699,747,912,931,965,1092,1131,
1136,1403

advertisement (advertisement agency)
34,38,221,261,311,384,530,548,560,665,673,686,827,
864,995,1041,1090,1100,1101,1157,1182,1184,1205,1206,
1234,1288,1305,1467,1475,1513

travel (travel agencies)
813,814,872,876,954,1004,1043,1077,1241,1279,1358

resort
355,586,792,1124,1380

service industry
28,288,379,380,381,383,790,810,866,920,1444

galleries/museums
118,263,264,265,269,270,524,1180,1238,1274,1302,1315,
1542

design studios
86,161,184,207,218,235,280,321,329,345,354,357,414,
423,426,450,466,476,529,551,556,562,596,629,676,
677,819,1021,1125,1233,1303,1400,1411,1419,1563,1638

campaigns (festivals/exhibitions)
18,19,88,95,112,128,136,169,203,204,430,441,473,528,
536,558,591,630,631,638,652,703,727,737,885,904,962,
1013,1016,1029,1061,1115,1171,1227,1237,1249,1273,1276,
1287,1331,1337,1362,1488,1519,1568,1571,1572,1573,1602,
1605,1614,1652

private symbols
17,22,42,78,110,117,187,247,278,431,434,451,557,594,
609,759-761,779,780,781,1007,1153,1199,1431,1477,1478,
1505,1525,1524,1546,1600,1607,1635,1636

Yasaburo Kuwayama (About the Editor)

Yasaburo Kuwayama was born in Niigata prefecture, Japan in 1938. He graduated from the Musashino Art University in 1962 and taught typography at Asagaya Academie des Beaux-arts for five years. In 1969, he established the Kuwayama Design Room, and in 1970, he began teaching typography at the Musashino Art University. In 1972, he served as an "Examiner of Lettering", and in 1975, he taught lettering at the Asahi Culture Center; he also served as a permanent manager of the Japan Creative Finish Work Association at this time. Upon his retirement in 1979 from his positions in the Musashino Art University, The organization of Lettering Approval, the Asahi Culture Center, and the Japan Creative Finish Work Association, he was able to pursue other interests. At present, Kuwayama is a member of the Association du Typographique Internationale (A. TYP.), the Japan Typography Association (JTA), the Federation of German Typographers (BOB), the Tokyo Designers Space (TDS), and the Japan Graphic Designer Association (JAGDA). He is a member of the Jehovah Witness Christian Faith. His main books include 'Lettering & Design', 'Typeface Design' and 'Graphic Elements of The World'.

Editor : Yasaburo Kuwayama／Publisher : Kashiwashobo

1985-1991 Works Being Solicited
Marks, Symbols, Logotypes, Pictograms, Signs, Typefaces

Many marks, symbols, logotypes, pictograms and typefaces are designed every year, but what is the role that they play ? In order to find an answer to this question, marks, symbols, logotypes, pictograms, signs and typefaces are being solicited from designers for publication in a book.

Instead of just a record of works, this book will provide abundant material for reference in design, in searching for similar works, and in research. Since publication of an international edition is being planned, this book will undoubtedly benefit design circles throughout the world.

● **Works Solicited**
1. Marks, Symbols
2. Logotypes
3. Pictograms, Signs
4. Typefaces
5. Below you'll find instructions for application to the above mentioned categories.
   * Attach a photograph to works used in a special way or which develop in a special way. For example, those which change or move.
   * Specify special points.

● **Period** Works designed and used from 1985 to 1991
   * Includes works redesigned during this period

● **Size**
1. Marks, Symbols :   about 4 cm
2. Logotypes :   about 9 cm
3. Pictograms, Signs :   about 3 cm
4. Typefaces :   Height of one word about 2 cm
   * Other sizes are acceptable.
   * Paste the work on the application slip.
   * When submitting color photographs please use positive film. If black and white film, please send 5×7" prints.
   * Printed matter can be submitted.
   * For works that you want returned, write "R" in red.
   * Attach application slips to examples of the designer's work.
   * In cases where pictograms, signs and typefaces make up sets, paste the works on pasteboard and an application slip on the pasteboard.

● **Category** Circle one of the following :
1. Marks, symbols
2. Logotypes
3. Pictograms, Signs
4. Typefaces

● **Points to be Noted**
1. Motif or Production Aim (less than 30 words)
2. Business Category
3. Name of the Art Director(s)
4. Name of the Designer(s) (including colleagues)
5. Client
6. Year and Place Designed
7. Color (attach color samples or color proofs)
   * Write in English as much as possible
   * When writing by hand, please write clearly

● **Deadline** March 1, 1992

● **Send to** Kuwayama Design Room
1-3-1-501 Higashi Izumi, Komae-shi, Tokyo 201, Japan

   * Ask for or make copies if you want more application slips.
   * No application charge is required, but payment will not be made for works submitted.

* Works will not be returned (color positives will be returned).
* Some works may not be included in the book due to editing considerations.
* There are no qualifications or restrictions on the number of works submitted.
The following works cannot be included in the book.
* Works already included in this series.
* Works with no application slip attached or with inadequate entries on the application slip.
* Works which are inadequate as block copy.

Editor   Yasaburo Kuwayama
Member, Japan Typography Association (JTA)
Member, International Typography Association (ATYPI)
Member, Japan Graphic Designers Association (JAGDA)
Member, Tokyo Designers Space (TDS)
Special Member, BDB of West Germany

Publisher   Kashiwashobo
1-13-14 Honkomagome, Bunkyo-ku, Tokyo 113
Tel (03) 947-8254

Book Size A4, about 480 pages, 3 to 5 volumes Publication
Date approximately April 1989

Paste Monochrome Work

Application Slip

Circle one of following: 1.Mark, Symbol 2.Logotype 3.Pictogram 4.Typeface

1. Motif or production aim

2. Business Category(or Use Contents)

3. Art Director

4. Designer

5. Client

6. Year and Place Designed

7. Color

* On reverse side, fill applicant's name, address and phone number.